Math in Focus®

Singapore Math®
by Marshall Cavendish

Student Edition

Program Consultant and Author
Dr. Fong Ho Kheong

Authors
Chelvi Ramakrishnan
Michelle Choo

Marshall Cavendish
Education

U.S. Distributor

Houghton Mifflin Harcourt.
The Learning Company

Grade
1A

Contents

Chapter

2 Addition and Subtraction Within 10

Chapter Opener   **47**

? How can you tell if a number sentence is true or false?

RECALL PRIOR KNOWLEDGE   **48**
Counting

Hands-on Activity

Chapter

3 Shapes and Patterns

Chapter Opener   137

? What shapes do you see around you?
  How can you tell them apart?

RECALL PRIOR KNOWLEDGE   138

Recognizing shapes • Patterns

▶ Hands-on Activity

Chapter

4 Numbers to 20

Hands-on Activity

▶ Hands-on Activity

Chapter

6 Numbers to 40

Chapter Opener

? How can you keep track of a large number of objects?
How can you use place value to help you?

Counting on from 10 to 20 • Making a 10, and then counting on • Reading place-value charts • Comparing and ordering numbers • Number patterns

▶ Hands-on Activity

Calendar and Time

▶ Hands-on Activity

Manipulative List

10–sided die

Attribute block tray

Base-ten blocks

Base-ten unit

Base-ten rod

Clock

Connecting cubes

Craft sticks

Geoboards

Geometric solids

Math balance

Transparent counters

Preface

Welcome!

Math in Focus® is a program that puts **you** at the center of an exciting learning experience! This experience is all about helping you to really understand math and become a strong and confident problem solver!

What is in your book?

Each chapter in this book begins with a real-world example of the math topic you are about to learn.

In each chapter, you will see these features:

THINK provides a problem for the whole section, to get you thinking. If you cannot answer the problem right away, you can come back to it a few times as you work through the section.

ENGAGE contains tasks that link what you already know with what you will be learning next. You can explore and discuss the tasks with your classmates.

LEARN introduces you to new math concepts using examples and activities, where you can use objects to help you learn.

Hands-on Activity gives you the chance to work closely with your classmates, using objects or drawing pictures, to help you learn math.

TRY gives you the chance to practice what you are learning, with support.

INDEPENDENT PRACTICE allows you to work on different kinds of problems, and to use what you have learned to solve these problems on your own.

Additional features include:

RECALL PRIOR KNOWLEDGE	Math Talk	MATH SHARING	GAME
Helps you recall related concepts you learned before, accompanied by practice questions	Invites you to talk about your thinking and communicate your ideas to your classmates and teachers	Encourages you to create strategies, discover methods, and share them with your classmates and teachers using mathematical language	Helps you to really master the concepts you learned, through fun partner games
LET'S EXPLORE	**MATH JOURNAL**	**PUT ON YOUR THINKING CAP!**	**CHAPTER WRAP-UP**
Extends your learning through investigation	Allows you to reflect on your learning when you write down your thoughts about the concepts learned	Challenges you to apply the concepts to solve problems in different ways	Summarizes your learning in a flow chart and helps you to make connections within the chapter
CHAPTER REVIEW	**Assessment Prep**	**PERFORMANCE TASK**	**STEAM**
Provides you with a lot of practice in the concepts learned	Prepares you for state tests with assessment-type problems	Assesses your learning through problems that allow you to demonstrate your understanding and knowledge	Promotes collaboration with your classmates through interesting projects that allow you to use math in creative ways

Let's begin your exciting learning journey with us! Are you ready?

Chapter 1 Numbers to 10

One, two, three, four,
Hear the mighty ocean roar!
Five, six, seven, eight,
Time to play, so don't be late!
What's next?
Nine and ten.
Let's start all over again!

How many children are there?

How can you compare two numbers?

Name: _____   Date: _____

Counting

The toys are matched to show the same number.

▶ **Quick Check**

Find the toys that show the same number. Draw lines to match.

 1

 • •

 • •

 • •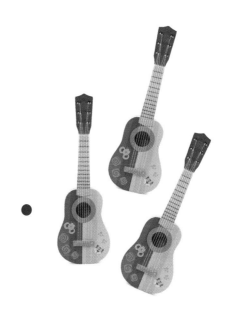

Find the shapes that show the same number.
Draw lines to match.

 • •

 • •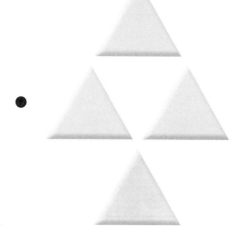

 • •

Counting to 10

Learning Objectives:
- Count on from 0 to 10.
- Understand the concept of zero by counting back.
- Read and write 0 to 10 in numbers and words.

 **THINK**

Count to find the numbers in the blanks.

1 1, ___, ___, 4, ___, ___, 7, ___

2 10, ___, ___, 7, ___, ___, 4, ___

Talk about how you count with your partner.

ENGAGE

1 Put some 🎲 on a ⊞.
Ask your partner to tell how many 🎲 you have.

2 Take 10 🔵.
Use a cup to cover some of them.
Ask your partner to find how many 🔵 are under the cup.

LEARN Count to 10

1

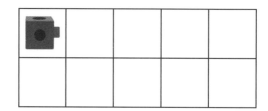

0
zero

1
one

2
two

3
three

4
four

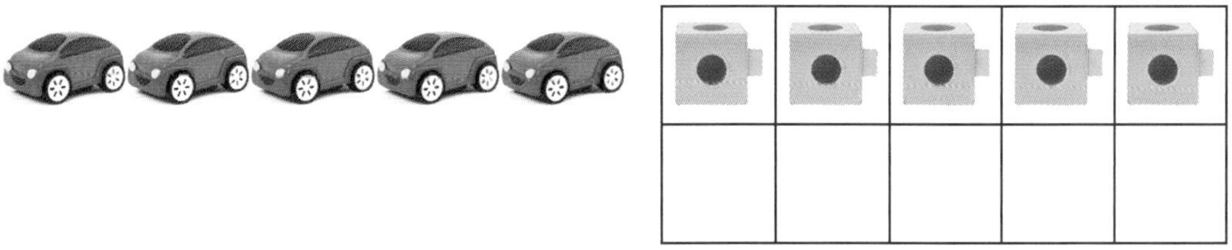

5
five

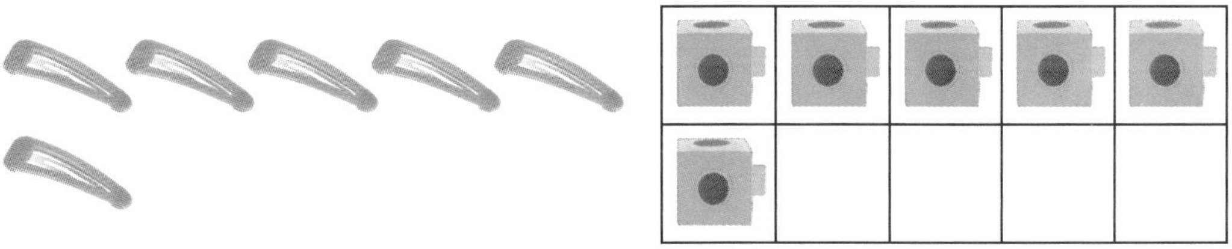

6
six

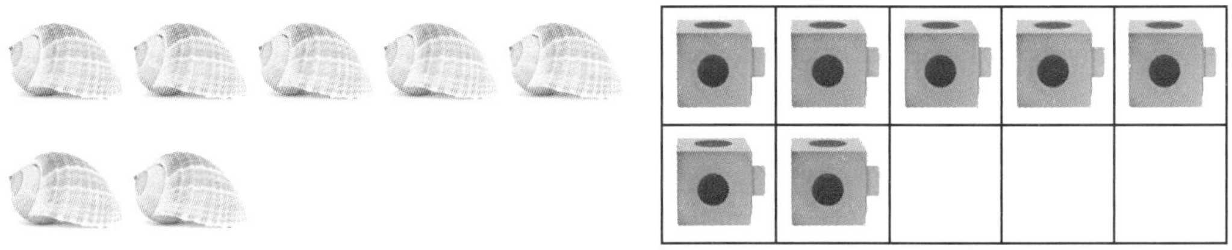

7
seven

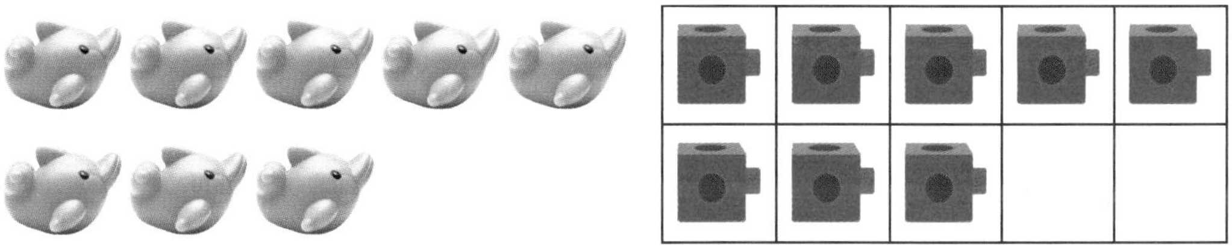

8
eight

9
nine

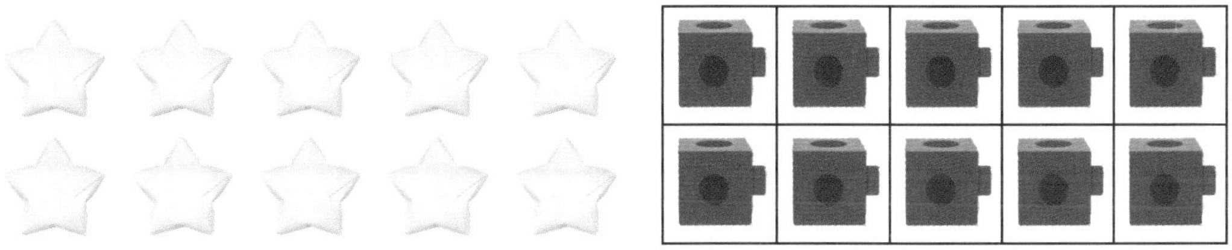

10
ten

Hands-on Activity

Take some **.**

Activity 1   Counting to 10

① Count the 🟦 on the ☐☐☐☐☐.
Place a 🟦 on the ☐☐☐☐☐ as you count.

Write the number. _____

② Repeat ① for these pictures.

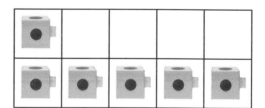

_____   _____

Activity 2   Showing numbers to 10

① Put eight 🟦 on a ☐☐☐☐☐.

② Repeat ① for 10 🟦.

TRY Practice counting to 10

Color to show seven.

1

Count.
Then, write each number.

2

_____

3

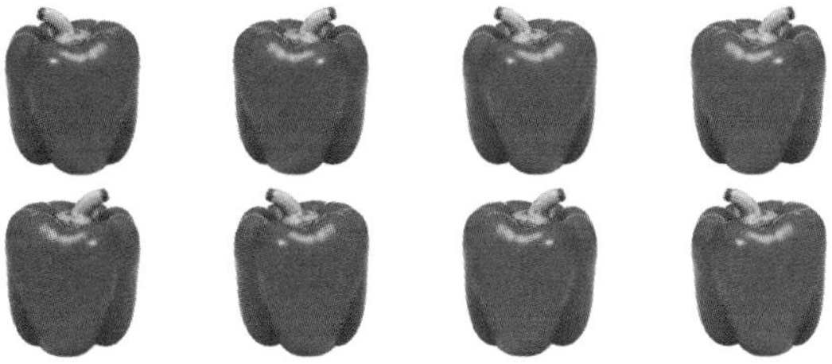

_____

4

_____

5

_____

6 **Draw lines to match each number and word.**

ENGAGE

1 Use  to show this story:
There are three apples on a plate.
Austin ate one.
Then, Pedro ate one.
Then, Layla ate one.
How many apples are left?

2 Your teacher will give you a bag of 🐝.
Guess how many 🐝 there are in it.
Take the 🐝 out and count back from your guess.
How do you know if your guess is correct?

LEARN Count back to 0

1 Point to the bees and count.

2

3

1

0

Hands-on Activity Counting back to 0

① Take five 🔲.

② Take away one 🔲.
How many 🔲 are left?
Write the number in the table below.

③ Take away another 🔲.
How many 🔲 are left now?
Write the number in the table below.

④ Repeat ③ until there are no 🔲 left.

Number of 🔲	Take away	Number of 🔲 left
5	1	
	1	

TRY Practice counting back to 0

Circle the plate with 0 apples.

1

Make an ✗ until there are 0 fruit left.

2

3

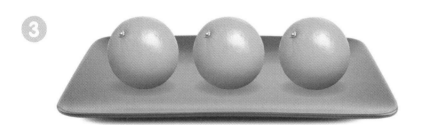

4

MATCH UP!

It is a match!

What you need:

Players: 2
Materials: Number cards, Word cards

What to do:

Place the cards face down on the table.

1 Player 1 turns over a number and a word card.
Keep the cards if they match.
Turn them back if they do not.

2 Trade places.
Repeat 1.

Who is the winner?

The first player to collect ten cards wins.

INDEPENDENT PRACTICE

Count.
Then, write each number.

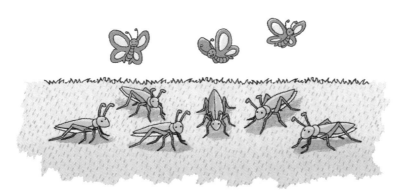

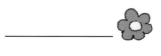

Count.
Then, write each number and word.

4

© 2020 Marshall Cavendish Education Pte Ltd

Comparing Numbers

Learning Objectives:
- Compare two sets of objects by using one-to-one correspondence.
- Tell if two sets have the same number of objects.
- Find the set that has more or fewer objects.
- Find the number that is greater than or less than another number.

New Vocabulary
same
as many as
more
fewer

THINK

Isabel is 3 years old.
Logan is 10 years old.
Anna is older than Isabel but younger than Logan.
How old could Anna be?
How do you know?
Share your thinking with your partner.

ENGAGE

Take some ▪.
Put them in a row.
Take fewer ▪ than ▪.
Put the ▪ in another row.
Take more ▪ than ▪.
Are there more ▪ or ▪?

LEARN Match and compare

1

There are four children.
There are four apples.

The number of children and the number of apples are the **same**.

There are **as many** children **as** apples.

2

There are four children.
There are three apples.

There are **more** children than apples.
There are **fewer** apples than children.

Hands-on Activity Matching and comparing sets of objects

Your teacher will give you two ☐☐☐☐☐☐☐☐☐☐.

① Take some ⬤ and ◯.
Place all the ⬤ on one ☐☐☐☐☐☐☐☐.
Place all the ◯ on another ☐☐☐☐☐☐☐☐.

② Match and compare the number of ⬤ and ◯.
Write **more** or **fewer**.

a There are _____ ⬤ than ◯.

b There are _____ ◯ than ⬤.

③ Repeat ① and ②.
Use a different number of ⬤ and ◯.

a There are _____ ⬤ than ◯.

b There are _____ ◯ than ⬤.

TRY Practice matching and comparing

Match and compare.
Then, write more or fewer.

There are _____  than .

There are _____ 🦋 than 🌼.

There are _____ 🐱 than 🐟.

There are _____ 🦆 than 🐟.

More or fewer?

ENGAGE

a Put four  on your mat.
   Write 4.

b Now, put six  on your mat.
   Write 6.

c Do you have more  or ?

d Take more  than  but fewer than .
   How many  did you take?

LEARN Count and compare

1  ········ 5

    ············· 3

There are more  than .
So, 5 is greater than 3.

There are fewer  than .
So, 3 is less than 5.

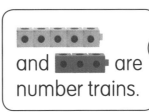
and are number trains.

How can you compare 5 and 3 without using ?

3, 4, 5, …
5 comes after 3.
So, 5 is greater than 3.

Hands-on Activity Comparing numbers

Take some .

① Make number trains for these numbers.

9   4

② Compare 4 and 9.
Which number is greater? _____

Which number is less? _____

③ Repeat ① and ② for these numbers.
Then, answer each question.

a   7   4

Which number is greater, 7 or 4? _____

b   6   9

Which number is less, 6 or 9? _____

TRY Practice counting and comparing

Fill in each blank.

1.  _____

    _____

   _____ is greater than _____.

   _____ is less than _____.

2. 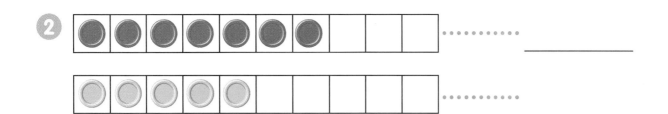 _____

   _____ is greater than _____.

   _____ is less than _____.

3.

   _____ is greater than _____.

   _____ is less than _____.

COMPARE THEM!

What you need:

Players: 2
Materials: Picture cards

What to do:

Place the cards face down on the table.

1. Player 1 turns over two cards.
   Compare the cards using these words.

   | more | fewer | the same |

2. Player 2 checks the answer.
   A correct answer receives one point.

3. Trade places.
   Repeat 1 and 2.

Who is the winner?

The player with more points after five rounds wins.

INDEPENDENT PRACTICE

Circle.

1 Which two groups show the same number?

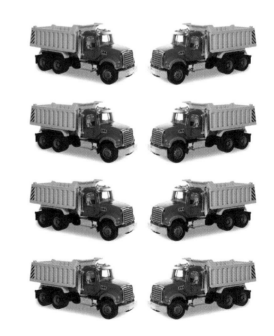

Fill in each blank.

2 Which tank has more fish?

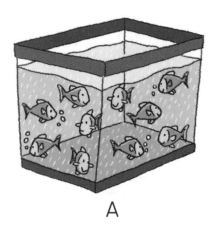 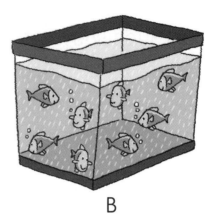

A   B

Tank _____ has more fish.

3 Which box has fewer chicks?

 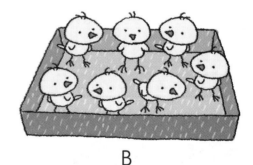

A   B

Box _____ has fewer chicks.

Write the greater number.

4 2 or 4 _____   **5** 7 or 3 _____

Write the number that is less.

6 9 or 8 _____   **7** 5 or 6 _____

3 Number Patterns

Learning Objectives:
- Find 1 more or 1 less than a number.
- Find the missing numbers in a number pattern.

New Vocabulary
more than
less than

 **THINK**

Count to find the numbers in the blanks.

1 ___, ___, ___, 4, ___, ___, 7, ___

2 ___, ___, ___, 6, ___, ___, 3, ___

Talk about how you count with your partner.

ENGAGE

1 Use 🧊 to show this story:
A train has 4 cars.
1 more car hooked up to the train.
How many cars does the train have now?

2 Bailey makes a train with 🧊.
She adds 🧊 to the front and back of the train, one at a time.
In the end, there are 10 🧊 in the train.
How many 🧊 did Bailey start with?
What are some likely numbers?

LEARN Find 1 more or 1 less than a number

1 What is 1 more than 3?

3

1 more

4 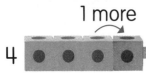   4 is 1 more than 3.

2 What is 1 less than 4?

4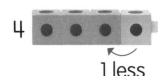

1 less

3 ● ● ●   3 is 1 less than 4.

Hands-on Activity Using 🧊 to find 1 more or 1 less than a number

Take some 🧊.

① Use these 🧊 to make a number train.
How many 🧊 are there in your number train? _____

② What number is 1 more and 1 less than the number of 🧊 in your number train?

_____ is 1 more than _____.

_____ is 1 less than_____.

TRY Practice finding 1 more or 1 less than a number

Fill in each blank.

1 _____ is 1 more than 5.

2 _____ is 1 less than 5.

Count.
Then, fill in each blank.

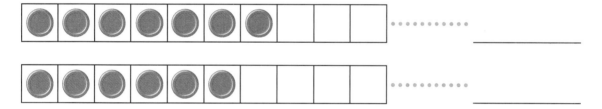

3 _____ is 1 less than _____.

4 _____ is 1 more than _____.

ENGAGE

1 Use 🎲 to make these number trains:
   1 cube, 2 cubes, 3 cubes, 4 cubes, 5 cubes, 6 cubes,
   7 cubes, 8 cubes
   How many 🎲 will there be in the next number train?

2 Make number trains to make other patterns.
   Talk about how you came up with the numbers with your
   partner.

LEARN Find missing numbers in a number pattern

1 Molly uses 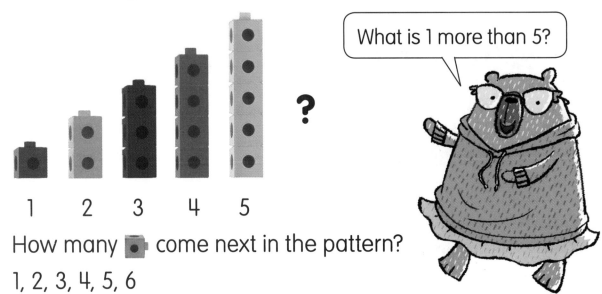 to make the pattern below.

?

What is 1 more than 5?

1 2 3 4 5

How many come next in the pattern?

1, 2, 3, 4, 5, 6

6 come next in the pattern.

2 William uses ◯ to make a pattern.

◯◯◯◯◯◯◯◯ 8

◯◯◯◯◯◯◯ 7

◯◯◯◯◯◯ 6

◯◯◯◯◯ 5

What is 1 less than 5?

How many ◯ come next in the pattern?

8, 7, 6, 5, 4

4 ◯ come next in the pattern.

Take some 🧊.

① **Mathematical Habit 8** Look for patterns

Use 🧊 to show a pattern from 3 to 7.

Example:

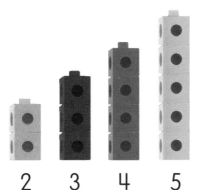

This shows a pattern from 2 to 5.

2   3   4   5

② **Mathematical Habit 8** Look for patterns

Use 🧊 to show a pattern from 9 to 5.

TRY Practice finding missing numbers in a number pattern

Solve.

① Rosie makes a pattern with beads.

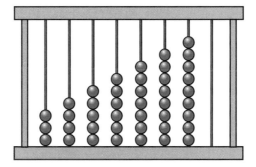

How many beads come next in the pattern? _____

2 Write each missing number in the number pattern.

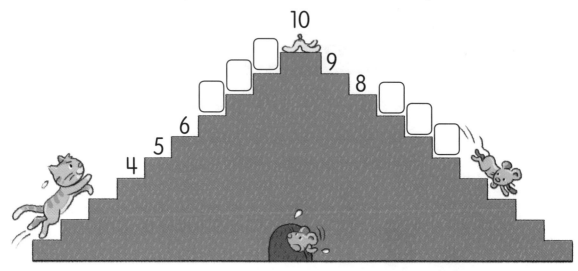

1 Make a number train with more than five 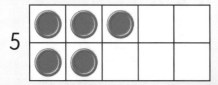.
How many 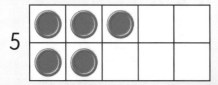 are there in your train?
Can you do it in a different way?

2 Make a number train with fewer than five 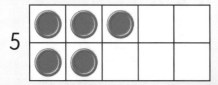.
How many 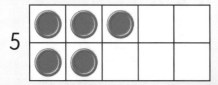 are there in your train?
Can you do it in a different way?

3 Pick a number from 2 to 9.
Use 🟢 to show your number on a ▭▭▭▭▭.
Show your number in different ways
on the ▭▭▭▭▭.
Example:

5

●	●	●		
●	●			

or

●	●	●	●	
●				

INDEPENDENT PRACTICE

Fill in each blank.

1 What is 1 more than 8?

_____ is 1 more than 8.

2 What is 1 less than 6?

_____ is 1 less than 6.

3 _____ is 1 less than 10.

4 1 less than 3 is _____.

5 Count on.
Find the next number in the number pattern.

1, 2, 3, 4, _____

How many 😊 come next in the pattern?
Draw them.

6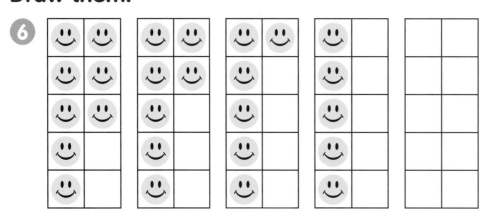

Write the missing numbers in each number pattern.

7

1 2 3 4   7

8

   5 6 7 8

9

8   5 4 3 2

10

6 5 4 3

Mathematical Habit 3 **Construct viable arguments**

Which sentences are correct?
Write or draw to show your thinking.

a   A bicycle has two wheels.

b   A cat has four legs.

c   5 is greater than 7.

d   8 is less than 9.

Problem Solving with Heuristics

Here are some counters.

1 **Mathematical Habit 3** Construct viable arguments

a   Group the numbers this way.

Numbers less than 5	Numbers from 5 to 7	Numbers greater than 7

b   What can you say about the counters in each group?

2 **Mathematical Habit 3** Construct viable arguments

a   Write all the numbers greater than 2 but less than 9.

b   Use five of the numbers in **a** to make two number patterns.
Describe each number pattern you make.

CHAPTER WRAP-UP

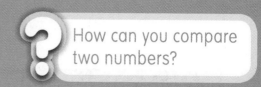

How can you compare two numbers?

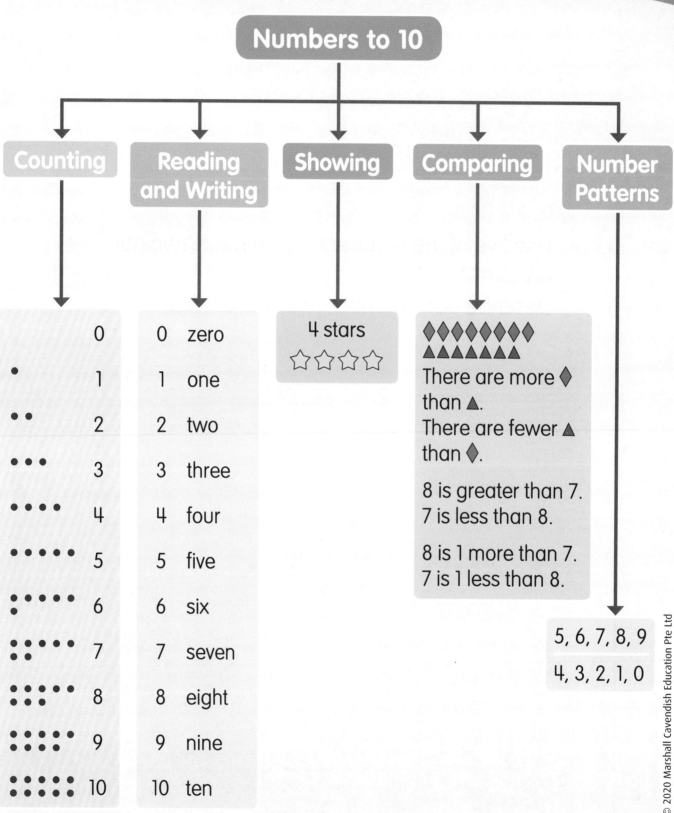

Numbers to 10

Counting

	0
•	1
••	2
•••	3
••••	4
•••••	5
••••••	6
•••••••	7
••••••••	8
•••••••••	9
••••••••••	10

Reading and Writing

0	zero
1	one
2	two
3	three
4	four
5	five
6	six
7	seven
8	eight
9	nine
10	ten

Showing

4 stars
☆☆☆☆

Comparing

◆◆◆◆◆◆◆◆
▲▲▲▲▲▲▲

There are more ◆ than ▲.
There are fewer ▲ than ◆.

8 is greater than 7.
7 is less than 8.

8 is 1 more than 7.
7 is 1 less than 8.

Number Patterns

5, 6, 7, 8, 9

4, 3, 2, 1, 0

Name: _____   Date: _____

Count.
Then, write each number and word.

Number _____

Word _____

Number _____

Word _____

Number _____

Word _____

Which group has more ?
Circle.

④

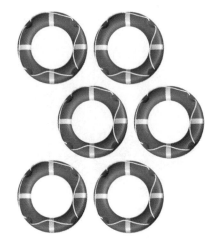

Which group has fewer ?
Circle.

⑤

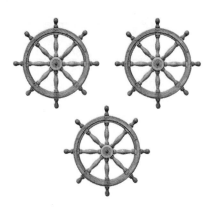

Which number is less?
Color.

 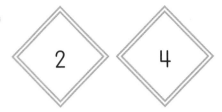

Which number is greater?
Color.

Fill in each blank.

10 _____ is 1 more than 1.

11 _____ is 1 less than 1.

Write the missing numbers in each number pattern.

12

13

Assessment Prep
Answer each question.

14 Which group shows 7?

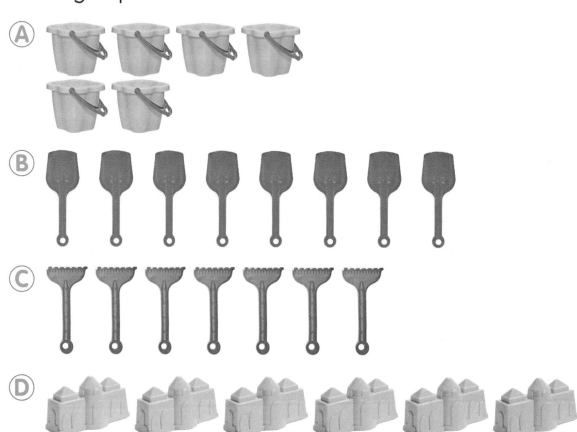

15 Color the numbers that are greater than 5.

 7   4   5   6

Name: _____ Date: _____

A Day at the Beach

1 Some children are playing volleyball.
How many children are there?
Write the number and word.

Number _____   Word _____

2 The Jones family is having a picnic.
How many people are there?
Write the number and word.

Number _____   Word _____

3 Carla sees some seashells on the seashore.

Draw ● to show the number of seashells she sees.

4 Count.
Then, write each number.

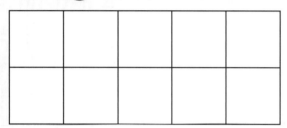 _____

 _____

_____ is greater than _____.

_____ is less than _____.

5 Fill in each blank.

a _____ is 1 more than 9.

b _____ is 1 less than 9.

6 Write the missing number in each number pattern.

a

b

Rubric

Point(s)	Level	My Performance
7–8	4	• Most of my answers are correct. • I show all my work correctly. • I explain my thinking clearly and completely.
5–6.5	3	• Some of my answers are correct. • I show some of my work correctly. • I explain my thinking clearly.
3–4.5	2	• A few of my answers are correct. • I show little work correctly. • I explain some of my thinking clearly.
0–2.5	1	• A few of my answers are correct. • I show little or no work. • I do not explain my thinking clearly.

Teacher's Comments

How can you tell if a number sentence is true or false?

Name: _____ Date: _____

Counting

a   There are five .

1   2   3   4   5

b      1 more

6 is 1 more than 5.

c

6 is 1 less than 7.

1 less

▶ **Quick Check**

Count.
Then, write the number.

    _____

Count to find each missing number.

2   2, 3, 4, 5, _____, _____, _____

3   10, 9, 8, 7, _____, _____, _____

Making Number Bonds

Learning Objectives:
- Use connecting cubes or a math balance to make number bonds.
- Make number bonds for numbers to 10.

New Vocabulary
number bonds
part
whole

THINK

Complete the number bond for each sentence.

1 7 and _____ make 9.

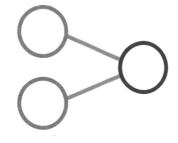

2 5 and _____ make 8.

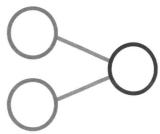

ENGAGE

Use  to make a number train of 6.

Close your eyes and break the number train into two parts.

What are the different ways you can do this?

Draw a sketch of each way.

How many 🧊 are in each number train?

1 Maya breaks into two parts.

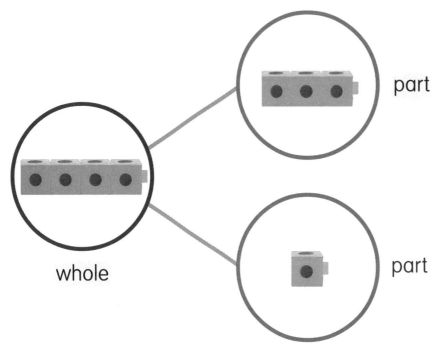

part

whole

part

How many are in each part?

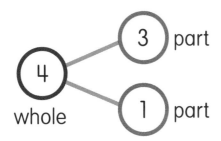

3 part

4
whole

1 part

3 and 1 make 4.
This is a number bond.

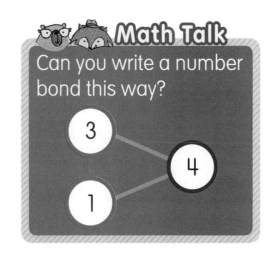

Math Talk

Can you write a number bond this way?

3

4

1

Hands-on Activity

Activity 1   Using to make number bonds of 4

① Use to make number bonds of 4.
What other numbers make 4?

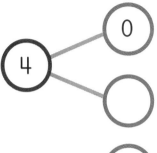

_____ and _____ make 4.

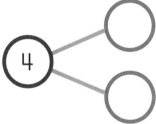

_____ and _____ make 4.

Activity 2   Using to make number bonds of 5

① Use to make number bonds of 5.
What numbers make 5?

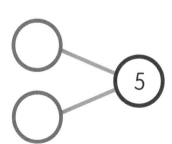   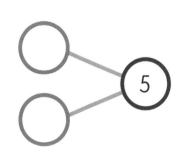   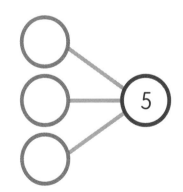

TRY Practice using 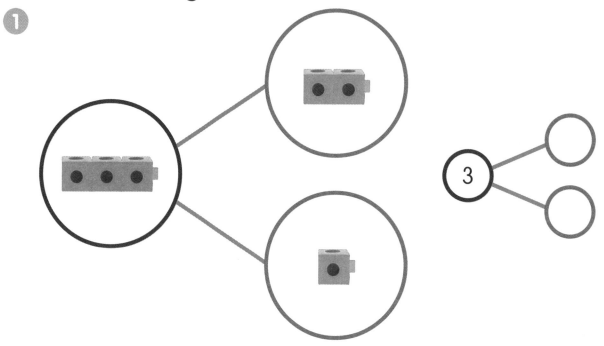 to make number bonds

Write each missing number.

1

2 and 1 make _____.

Draw ☐ to complete the number bond.
Then, write each missing number.

2

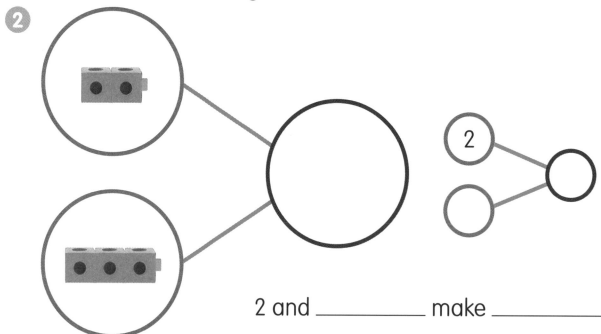

2 and _____ make _____.

ENGAGE

Watch your teacher put a 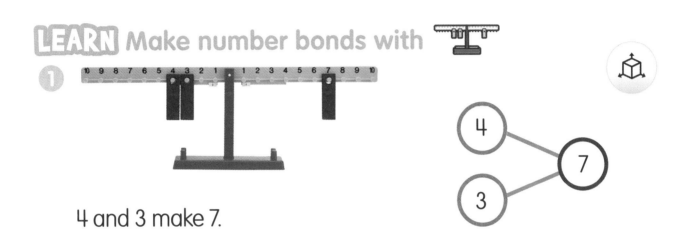 on one side of a ⚖ .
Now, watch your classmate put two ▯ on the other side.
Where else can you place the ▯?
Share your thinking with your classmates.

LEARN Make number bonds with ⚖

1

4 and 3 make 7.

Hands-on Activity Using ⚖ to make number bonds

1 Use ⚖ to make number bonds of 7.
What other numbers make 7?

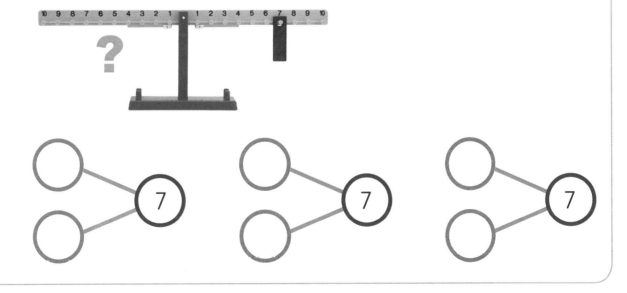

TRY Practice using 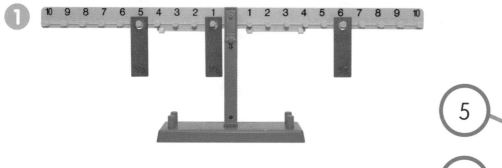 to make number bonds

Write each missing number.

1

5 and 1 make _____.

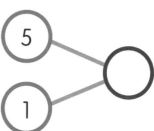

Draw each missing 🔲.
Then, write each missing number.

2

4 and 2 make _____.

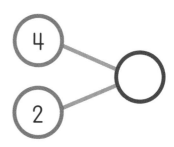

3
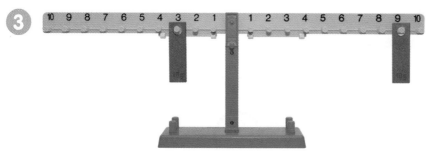

3 and _____ make 9.

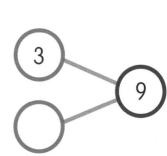

INDEPENDENT PRACTICE

Look at each picture.
Then, complete each number bond.

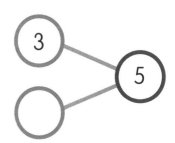

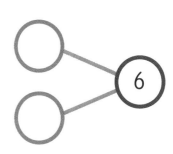

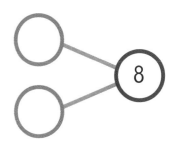

Complete each number bond.

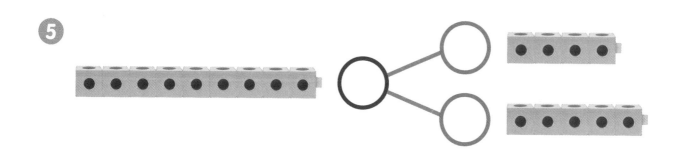

Write each missing number.
Use 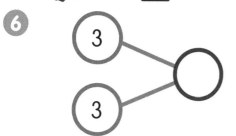 or ![balance] to help you.

6

3 and 3 make _____.

7

6 and 2 make _____.

8

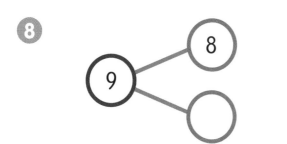

8 and _____ make 9.

9

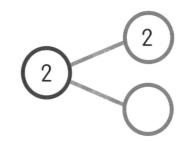

2 and _____ make 2.

2 Ways to Add

Learning Objectives:
- Add using number bonds.
- Add by counting on.
- Write and solve addition sentences.

THINK

Look at the addition sentence.

$2 + 5 +$ _____ $= 10$

What is the missing number?
Talk about how you get the answer with your partner.

ENGAGE

1 Use  to show this story:
Samantha has 4 red flowers and 2 yellow flowers.
How many flowers does she have in all?

2 Adrian has 7 blue and green balls.
There are more blue balls than green balls.
How many blue balls does Adrian have?
How many green balls does he have?

There is more than one answer.

LEARN Add with number bonds

1 How many toy cars are there in all?

part (3)   whole

part (2)   (5)

3 + 2 = 5
There are 5 toy cars in all.

3 + 2 = 5 is an addition sentence.
You can read it as, "three plus two
is equal to five."

"+" is read as plus.
It means put together.

"=" is read as
is equal to.

2 How many lemons are there in all?

There are 8 lemons in all.

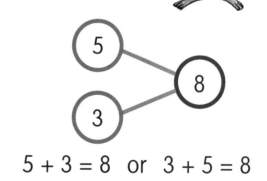

(5)
(3)   (8)

5 + 3 = 8 or 3 + 5 = 8

Math Talk
What do you notice about the
answers to "5 + 3" and "3 + 5"?

TRY Practice using number bonds to add

Add.
Use number bonds to help you.

① How many paper clips are there in all?

_____ + _____ = _____ or

_____ + _____ = _____

There are _____ paper clips in all.

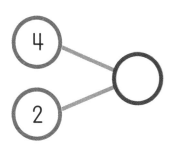

② How many monkeys are there in all?

_____ + _____ = _____ or

_____ + _____ = _____

There are _____ monkeys in all.

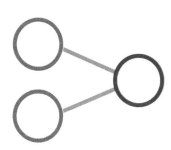

ENGAGE

1 Put 4 in a cup.

Ask your partner to put 3 in the cup, one at a time.

How many are in the cup now?

2 Fill in the blank.

5 + _____ = 9

LEARN Add by counting on

1 How many buttons are there in all?

6 buttons   2 buttons

6 + 2 = ?
Count on from the greater number to add.

6 + 2 = 8
There are 8 buttons in all.

8

2 steps   7

6

Math Talk

Why do you count on from the greater number?

2 How many cubes are there in all?

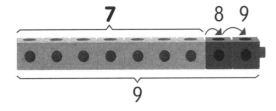

7   8   9

9

7 + 2 = 9
There are 9 cubes in all.

7, 8, 9

2 added to 7 is 9.

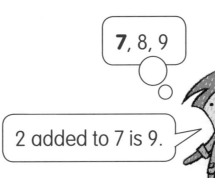

Hands-on Activity Counting on to add

Work in pairs.
Your teacher will give you a paper cup.

① Write a number on your cup.

② Take some .
You must take more than the number on the cup.

③ Place the number of you wrote in your cup.
Then, ask your partner to count on as he or she puts the rest of the into the cup.

TRY Practice counting on to add

Add.
Count on from the greater number.

① How many counters are there in all?
5 + 2 = ?

5, _____, _____

② How many cubes are there in all?

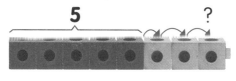

5 + 3 = _____

5, ____, ____, ____

ADD THEM UP!

The answer is 6.

4 + 2

Correct!

What you need:

Players: 2
Materials: Addition cards

What to do:

Place the cards face down on the table.

1 Player 1 turns over a card.

2 Player 2 adds the numbers on the card.

3 Player 1 then checks the answer.
A correct answer receives one point.

4 Trade places.
Repeat 1 to 3.

Who is the winner?

The player with more points after five rounds wins.

INDEPENDENT PRACTICE

Add.
Use number bonds to help you.

1 How many crayons are there in all?

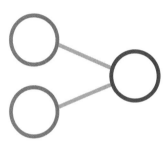

_____ + _____ = _____ or

_____ + _____ = _____

There are _____ crayons in all.

2 How many sheep are there in all?

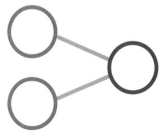

_____ + _____ = _____ or

_____ + _____ = _____

There are _____ sheep in all.

3 How many bees are there in all?

_____ + _____ = _____ or

_____ + _____ = _____

There are _____ bees in all.

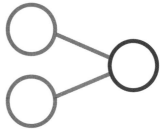

4 How many cubes are there in all?

_____ + _____ = _____ or

_____ + _____ = _____

There are _____ cubes in all.

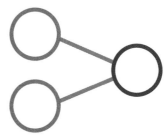

Add.
Count on from the greater number.

5

$4 + 2 = $ _____

6

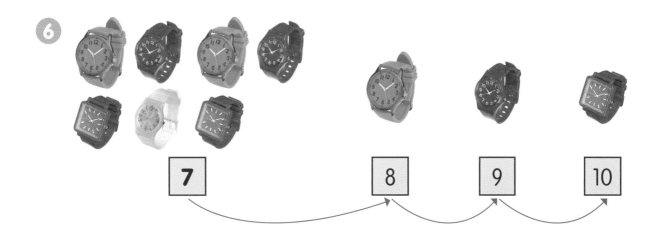

$7 + 3 = $ _____

7

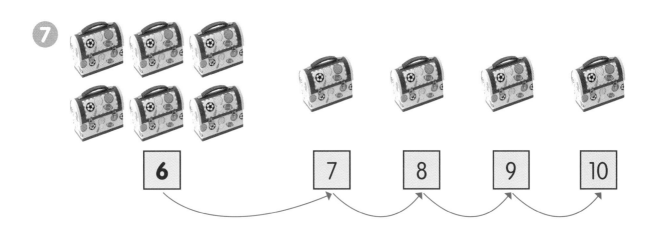

$6 + 4 = $ _____

Add.
Count on from the greater number.

8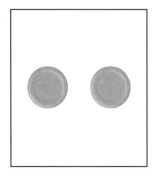

$2 + 1 =$ _____

9

$5 + 2 =$ _____

10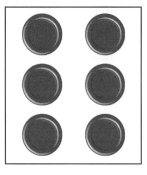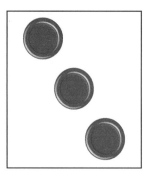

$6 + 3 =$ _____

Add.
Use the counting tape to help you.

1	2	3	4	5	6	7	8	9	10

11 $8 + 1 =$ _____   **12** $2 + 2 =$ _____

13 $3 + 3 =$ _____   **14** $3 + 5 =$ _____

3 Making Addition Stories

Learning Objectives:
- Make addition stories about pictures.
- Write and solve addition sentences related to addition stories.

THINK

Look at the picture.
Make two addition stories.
Then, write an addition sentence for each story.

ENGAGE

Take 3 🔲 and some 🔲 from 10 🔲.

Make an addition story about the 🔲 you took.

Tell your partner your story.

Then, ask your partner to write the addition sentence.

① Look at the picture.
Make an addition story.

5 ducks are in a pond.
4 ducks join them.

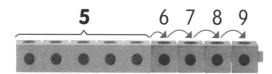

5   6 7 8 9

$5 + 4 = 9$
There are 9 ducks in all.

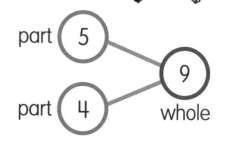

part 5

part 4

9 whole

Work in pairs.
Your teacher will give you some cards.
Each card has an addition sentence.

① Choose a card.
Do not show your partner.

② **Mathematical Habit 4** Use mathematical models

Make an addition story based on the addition sentence.

Use 🪙 to tell the story.

③ **Mathematical Habit 4** Use mathematical models

Ask your partner to write the addition sentence based on the story.

④ Trade places.
Repeat ① to ③.

Practice making addition stories

Look at each picture.
Make an addition story.
Then, write each missing number.

1

> One plate has ___ apples.
> The other plate has ___ apples.

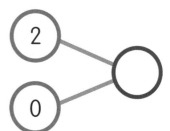

2 + 0 = _____

There are _____ apples in all.

2

> ___ girls are playing.
> ___ girl joins them.

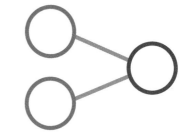

_____ + _____ = _____

There are _____ girls in all.

INDEPENDENT PRACTICE

Look at each picture.
Make an addition story.
Then, fill in each blank.

red hair bands   purple hair bands

There are _____ red hair bands.

There are _____ purple hair bands.

_____ ◯ _____ = _____

There are _____ hair bands in all.

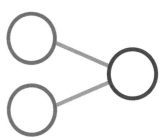

②

blue bow ties   black bow ties

Mr. Smith has _____ blue bow ties.

He has _____ black bow ties.

_____ ◯ _____ = _____

Mr. Smith has _____ bow ties in all.

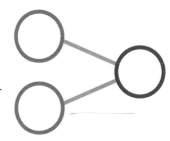

3

_____ frogs are in the pond.

_____ more frogs join them.

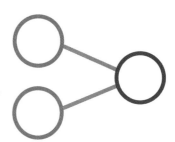

_____ ◯ _____ = _____

There are _____ frogs in all.

4

There are _____ roses in the vase.

June puts _____ more roses into the vase.

_____ ◯ _____ = _____

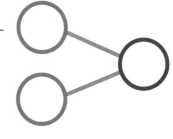

There are _____ roses in all.

Real-World Problems: Addition

Learning Objectives:
• Write addition sentences related to real-world problems.
• Solve real-world problems involving addition.

 THINK

Addison has three fish tanks.
She has 2 blue fish in each tank.
She also has 1 orange fish in two of the tanks.
How many fish does Addison have in all?

ENGAGE

There are two boxes of cookies.
There are 8 cookies in all.
How many cookies can there be in each box?
Use 🔵 to show two different ways.

Solve real-world problems involving addition

1 There are 6 chickens on a farm.
There are 3 ducks on the same farm.
How many animals are there in all?

STEP 1 Understand the problem.

How many chickens are there?
How many ducks are there?
What do I need to find?

STEP 2 Think of a plan.
I can use number bonds to help me add.

STEP 3 Carry out the plan.
6 + 3 = 9
There are 9 animals in all.

part 6
3 part
9 whole

STEP 4 Check the answer.
I can use 🎲 to help me
check my answer.

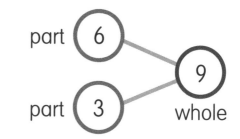

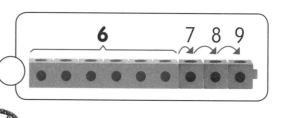

2 Jayla has 4 paper planes.
She makes 5 more paper planes.
How many paper planes does Jayla have now?

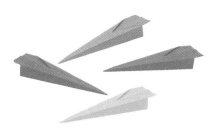
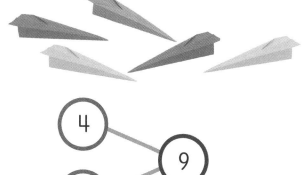

4 + 5 = 9
Jayla has 9 paper planes now.

TRY Practice solving real-world problems involving addition

Solve.

1 There are 2 blue fish in a tank.
There are also 4 orange fish in the same tank.
How many fish are there in all?

Use the four-step problem-solving model to help you.

_____ + _____ = _____

There are _____ fish in all.

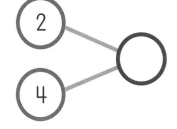

2 Antonio has 4 red markers.
He also has 3 blue markers.
How many markers does Antonio have in all?

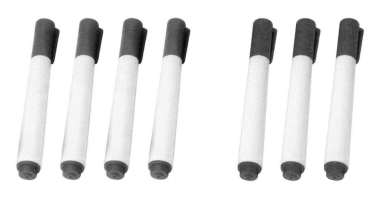

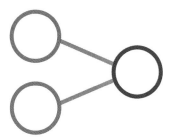

_____ + _____ = _____

Antonio has _____ markers in all.

3 There are no mushrooms on a plate.
John puts 4 mushrooms onto the plate.
How many mushrooms are there on the plate now?

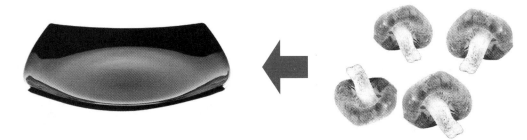

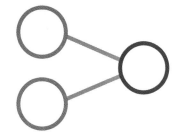

_____ + _____ = _____

There are _____ mushrooms on the
plate now.

INDEPENDENT PRACTICE

Solve.

1 A store sells 5 pink sweaters.
It also sells 3 blue sweaters.
How many sweaters does the shop sell in all?

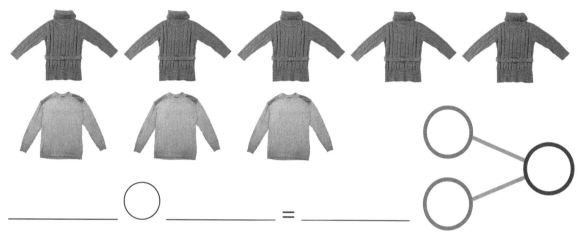

_____ ◯ _____ = _____

The shop sells _____ sweaters in all.

2 Ava paints 4 yellow flowers.
Mason paints 4 purple flowers.
How many flowers do the children paint in all?

_____ ◯ _____ = _____

The children paint _____ flowers in all.

3 Axel has 5 books.
He buys another 2 books.
How many books does Axel have now?

_____ ◯ _____ = _____

Axel has _____ books now.

4 Vijay folds 7 paper boats.
He then folds another 3 paper boats.
How many paper boats does Vijay fold in all?

_____ ◯ _____ = _____

Vijay folds _____ paper boats in all.

5 Ways to Subtract

Learning Objectives:
- Subtract by taking away.
- Subtract by counting on.
- Subtract by counting back.
- Subtract using number bonds.
- Write and solve subtraction sentences.

 **THINK**

Michelle has 5 crayons.
2 crayons are out of the box.
How many crayons are in the box?
Talk about how you find the answer with your partner.

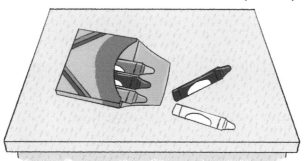

ENGAGE

a　Put 9 🧱 into a container.

　　Take 3 🧱 out.

　　How many 🧱 are left in the container?

b　Now, put all the 🧱 back into the container.

　　Take 5 🧱 out.

　　Ask your partner to take some 🧱 from the container.

　　What is the greatest number of 🧱 he or she can take?

LEARN Subtract by taking away

1 There are 9 goats.
6 goats walk away.
How many goats are left?

Crossing out 6 goats takes away 6 goats.

$$9 - 6 = 3$$

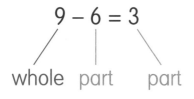

whole   part   part

"–" is read as minus.
It means subtract.

3 goats are left.

$9 - 6 = 3$ is a subtraction sentence.
It is read as, "nine minus six is equal to three."

2

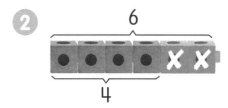

6

4

2 taken away from 6 is 4.

$$6 - 2 = 4$$
4 cubes are left.

Take some 🟤 **and a** ▦ **.**

① 9 − 3 = ?

Put 9 🟤 on the ▦ .

Then, take away 3 🟤 .

9 − 3 = _____

② Repeat ① for these subtraction sentences.

a   10 − 5 = _____   b   8 − 7 = _____

TRY Practice taking away to subtract

Write how many are left.

①

10 − 4 = _____

②

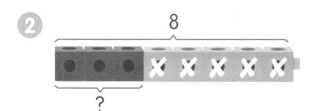

8 − 5 = _____

③

7 − 3 = _____

ENGAGE

Hold up 5 fingers.
How many more fingers do you need to hold up to get to 7?
Share two ways you can use to find the answer.

LEARN Subtract by counting on

1. 9 birds are on a wire.
   6 birds fly away.
   How many birds are left?

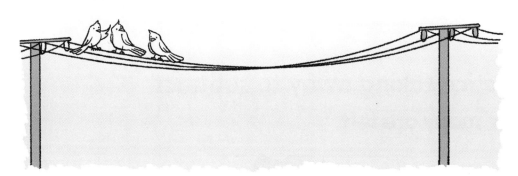

Find 9 – 6.
Count on from the number that is less, 6.
Stop at 9.

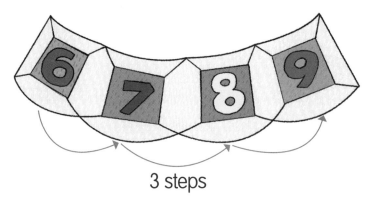

3 steps

6, 7, 8, 9

9 – 6 = 3
3 birds are left.

Work in groups of four.

① Take some .
Show them to your group.

② Next, hide some of the .

③ Ask your group to count on to find the number of hidden.

Now there are 5.

5, 6, 7, 8
You hid 3 .

There were 8.

Correct!

④ Check the answer.

⑤ Trade places.
Repeat ① to ④.

TRY Practice counting on to subtract

Subtract.
Count on from the number that is less.

1 How many leaves are left?

1	2	3	4	5	6	7	8

$8 - 6 =$ _____

_____ leaves are left.

Subtract.
Count on from the number that is less.
Use the counting tape to help you.

2 $6 - 3 =$ _____   3 $9 - 5 =$ _____

ENGAGE

Use [image] or [image] to show the following:

a Count back from 8 to show $8 - 6 =$ _____.

b Count back from 8 to show $8 - 2 =$ _____.

Which subtraction sentence is easier to solve using counting back?

Share your thinking with your partner.

LEARN Subtract by counting back

1. How many apples are left?

Start from the greater number, 9.
Count back 2 steps.

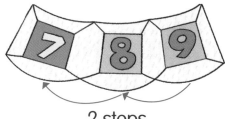

2 steps

 9 – 2 = ?

9, 8, 7

9 – 2 = 7
7 apples are left.

TRY Practice counting back to subtract

Subtract.
Count back from the greater number.

1. How many bananas are left?

7 – 2 = _____

_____ bananas are left.

| 1 | 2 | 3 | 4 | 5 | 6 | 7 |

2. 10 – 2 = _____   3. 9 – 3 = _____

ENGAGE

Draw number bonds to show this story:
Nolan wants to share 7 stickers with Madison.
What are the different ways Nolan can do this?
Write a subtraction sentence to show each way.

LEARN Subtract with number bonds

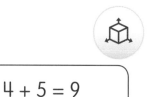

① How many beanbags is Alyssa holding?

9 – 4 = ?

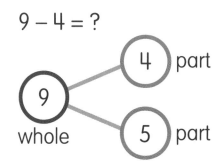

4 + 5 = 9
So, 9 – 4 = 5.

9 – 4 = 5
Alyssa is holding 5 beanbags.

② How many cherries are left on the plate?

5 – 1 = ?

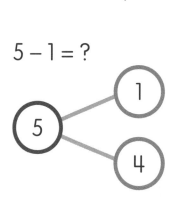

1 + 4 = 5
So, 5 – 1 = 4.

5 – 1 = 4
4 cherries are left on the plate.

TRY Practice using number bonds to subtract

Subtract.
Use number bonds to help you.

1 How many yellow beans are there?

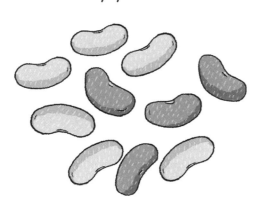

10 – _____ = _____

There are _____ yellow beans.

$4 +$ _____ $= 10$
So, $10 - 4 =$ _____.

2 How many fish do not swim away?

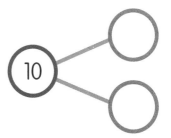

10 – _____ = _____

_____ fish do not swim away.

$3 +$ _____ $= 10$
So, $10 - 3 =$ _____.

SUBTRACT THEM!

Correct!

The answer is 4.

7-3

What you need:

Players: 2
Materials: Subtraction cards

What to do:

Place the deck of game cards face down.

1. Player 1 turns over a card.

2. Player 2 subtracts the numbers on the card.

3. Player 1 then checks the answer.
   A correct answer receives one point.

4. Trade places.
   Repeat 1 to 3.

Who is the winner?

The player with more points after five rounds wins.

INDEPENDENT PRACTICE

Cross out to subtract.
Then, fill in each blank.

1

10 – 2 = _____

2

8 – 2 = _____

3

9 – 3 = _____

4

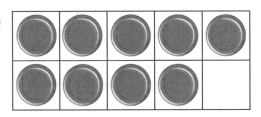

9 – 5 = _____

Subtract.
Count on from the number that is less.
Draw arrows to help you.

⑤ How many rabbits hop away?

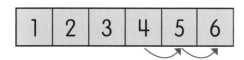

6 − 4 = _____

_____ rabbits hop away.

⑥ How many apples are left on the tree?

| 1 | 2 | 3 | 4 | 5 | 6 | 7 |

7 − 4 = _____

_____ apples are left on the tree.

7 How many butterflies fly away?

| 1 | 2 | 3 | 4 | 5 | 6 | 7 | 8 | 9 | 10 |

10 − 6 = _____

_____ butterflies fly away.

8 7 − 5 = _____

| 1 | 2 | 3 | 4 | 5 | 6 | 7 |

9 7 − 3 = _____

| 1 | 2 | 3 | 4 | 5 | 6 | 7 |

Subtract.
Count back from the greater number.
Draw arrows to help you.

10 How many cats are still drinking milk?

| 1 | 2 | 3 | 4 | 5 | 6 |

6 − 2 = _____

_____ cats are still drinking milk.

⑪ How many horses are still crossing the river?

| 1 | 2 | 3 | 4 | 5 | 6 | 7 |

7 – 1 = _____

_____ horses are still crossing the river.

⑫ How many crabs do not move away?

| 1 | 2 | 3 | 4 | 5 | 6 | 7 | 8 |

8 – 3 = _____

_____ crabs do not move away.

⑬ 8 – 2 = _____

| 1 | 2 | 3 | 4 | 5 | 6 | 7 | 8 |

⑭ 10 – 4 = _____

| 1 | 2 | 3 | 4 | 5 | 6 | 7 | 8 | 9 | 10 |

© 2020 Marshall Cavendish Education Pte Ltd

Fill in each blank.

15 How many frogs are on lily pads?

8 − _____ = _____

_____ frogs are on lily pads.

16 How many birds are left in the nest?

_____ − _____ = _____

_____ birds are left in the nest.

Complete each number bond.
Then, fill in each blank.

17 6 − 3 = ?

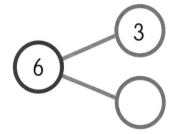

3 + _____ = 6

So, 6 − 3 = _____.

18 9 − 7 = ?

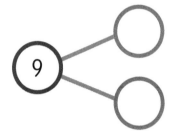

7 + _____ = 9

So, 9 − _____ = _____.

19 8 − 7 = ?

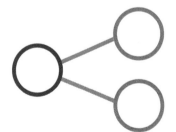

7 + _____ = 8

So, 8 − _____ = _____.

20 10 − 8 = ?

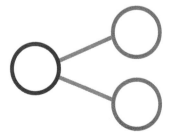

_____ + _____ = 10

So, 10 − _____ = _____.

6 Making Subtraction Stories

Learning Objectives:
- Make subtraction stories about pictures.
- Write and solve subtraction sentences related to subtraction stories.

THINK

Look at the picture.
Make two subtraction stories.
Then, write a subtraction sentence for each story.

ENGAGE

Put 10  in a cup.
Take some out.
Tell your partner your story.
Then, ask your partner to write the subtraction sentence.

LEARN Make subtraction stories about a picture

Look at each picture.

1 Make a subtraction story.

There are 7 animals.
4 of them are squirrels.

7 – 4 = 3
3 animals are hamsters.

Math Talk
What other subtraction story can you tell?

2 Make another subtraction story.

Laura has 10 apples.
Justin takes 2 apples from her.

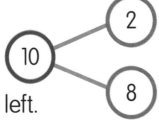

10 – 2 = 8
Laura has 8 apples left.

Work in pairs.
Your teacher will give you some cards.
Each card has a subtraction sentence.

(1) Choose a card.
Do not show your partner.

(2) **Mathematical Habit 4** Use mathematical models

Make a subtraction story based on the subtraction sentence.

Use to tell the story.

(3) **Mathematical Habit 4** Use mathematical models

Ask your partner to write the subtraction sentence based on the story.

(4) Trade places.
Repeat (1) to (3).

TRY Practice making subtraction stories

Look at each picture.
Make a subtraction story.
Then, find each missing number.

1

> There are ____ children.
> ____ of them wear glasses.

$4 -$ _____ $=$ _____

_____ children do not wear glasses.

2

Math Talk
What other subtraction story can you tell?

> There are ____ birds.
> ____ birds fly away.

_____ $-$ _____ $=$ _____

There are _____ birds left.

INDEPENDENT PRACTICE

Look at each picture.
Make a subtraction story.
Then, fill in each blank.

1

There are _____ pears.

Mr. Brown eats _____ pears.

_____ ◯ _____ = _____

There are _____ pears left.

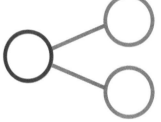

2

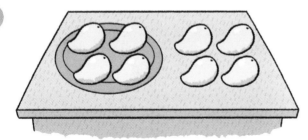

There are _____ mangoes in all.

_____ mangoes are on a plate.

_____ ◯ _____ = _____

_____ mangoes are not on the plate.

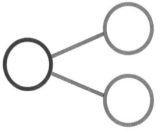

3

There are _____ eggs.

Gavin drops _____ eggs.

_____ ◯ _____ = _____

_____ eggs are left.

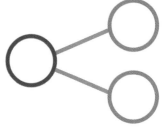

4

There are _____ bubbles.

Andrea pops _____ bubbles.

_____ ◯ _____ = _____

There are _____ bubbles left.

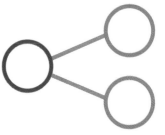

7 Real-World Problems: Subtraction

Learning Objectives:
- Write subtraction sentences related to real-world problems.
- Solve real-world problems involving subtraction.

THINK

There are 9 rabbits playing.
2 rabbits are brown.
The rest of the rabbits are white or gray.
After a while, the gray rabbits ran away.
How many gray rabbits ran away?

ENGAGE

1. James has 7 mangoes.

   He gives away some mangoes.

   He has 4 mangoes left.

   Use 🔵 to show how many mangoes James gives away.

2. Grayson has 7 red and green apples.

   He gives 2 apples to Luna.

   Grayson then has more red apples than green apples.

   How many more red apples than green apples does he have now?

   Give three answers.

LEARN Solve real-world problems involving subtraction

1. Lily and Grace have 9 oranges in all.
   Lily has 7 oranges.
   How many oranges does Grace have?

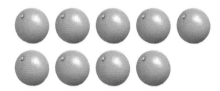

STEP 1 Understand the problem.

> How many oranges are there in all?
> How many oranges does Lily have?
> What do I need to find?

STEP 2 Think of a plan.
I can use number bonds to help me subtract.

STEP 3 Carry out the plan.
$9 - 7 = 2$
Grace has 2 oranges.

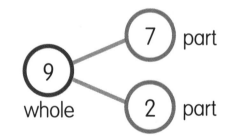

STEP 4 Check the answer.
I can use addition to help me check my answer.

$2 + 7 = 9$

2 There are 10 cherries.
Luis takes 6 cherries.
How many cherries are left?

$10 - 6 = 4$
4 cherries are left.

TRY Practice solving real-world problems involving subtraction

Solve.

1 There are 8 ants.
3 ants are black.
How many ants are red?

Use the four-step problem-solving model to help you.

_____ − _____ = _____

_____ ants are red.

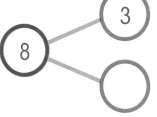

2 Stella has 9 balloons.
2 balloons burst.
How many balloons does Stella have left?

_____ − _____ = _____

Stella has _____ balloons left.

3 A tree has 7 lemons.
2 of the lemons are yellow.
How many lemons are green?

_____ − _____ = _____

_____ lemons are green.

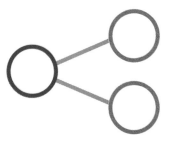

INDEPENDENT PRACTICE

Solve.

1 A shop is selling 5 fruit pies.
   2 are strawberry pies.
   How many apple pies are there?

_____ ◯ _____ = _____

There are _____ apple pies.

2 There are 9 apples.
   3 apples are red.
   How many green apples are there?

_____ ◯ _____ = _____

There are _____ green apples.

3 There are 8 shirts.
The wind blows a shirt away.
How many shirts are left?

_____ ◯ _____ = _____

_____ shirts are left.

4 There are 10 pies.
Elijah takes some.
8 pies are left.
How many pies does Elijah take?

_____ ◯ _____ = _____

Elijah takes _____ pies.

8 Making Fact Families

Learning Objectives:
- Recognize related addition and subtraction sentences.
- Write fact families.
- Use fact families to solve problems.
- Determine if number sentences involving addition and subtraction are true or false.

New Vocabulary
fact family
true
false

THINK

Fill in each box with the following.

| − | + | − | 3 | 5 | 9 |

6 ◯ ☐ = 9 ◯ ☐ = 0

◯ ☐ = 4

ENGAGE

Use 🎲 to make number bonds for 5.

Now, write two addition sentences.

Then, write two subtraction sentences.

Make and share a story for each addition and subtraction sentence.

LEARN Make fact families

1   orange ball

  green ball

How many balls are orange?
8 − 2 = 6

How many balls are green?
8 − 6 = 2

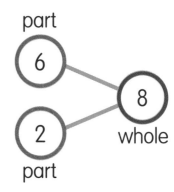

part
6
8
2   whole
part

How many balls are there in all?
2 + 6 = 8   or   6 + 2 = 8

2 8 − 2 = 6   8 − 6 = 2   2 + 6 = 8   6 + 2 = 8
This is a **fact family**.

Each fact in a fact family has the same parts and whole.

Hands-on Activity Making fact families with

Work in pairs.

① Take some and .

② **Mathematical Habit 7** **Make use of structure**

Ask your partner to write two addition and two subtraction sentences.

Example:

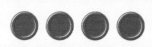

4 + 2 = 6 6 − 4 = 2

2 + 4 = 6 6 − 2 = 4

③ Trade places.

Repeat ① and ②.

__________ + __________ = __________

__________ + __________ = __________

__________ − __________ = __________

__________ − __________ = __________

TRY Practice making fact families

Make a fact family for each picture.

1

_____ + _____ = _____   _____ − _____ = _____

_____ + _____ = _____   _____ − _____ = _____

2

_____ + _____ = _____   _____ − _____ = _____

_____ + _____ = _____   _____ − _____ = _____

Write a fact family for these numbers.

3   10   2   8

_____ + _____ = _____   _____ − _____ = _____

_____ + _____ = _____   _____ − _____ = _____

ENGAGE

Some students were reading in a library.

3 students went home.

There are 4 students left in the library.

How many students were in the library at first?

Use  to help you solve the problem.

LEARN Use related facts to solve problems

1   Jess has some ●●.

She puts 5 ● in a bag.

3 ● are left.

How many ●● does Jess have?

I can use addition facts to solve subtraction sentences.

$$\underset{?}{\underline{\hspace{3cm}}} - 5 = 3$$

5 + 3 = 8 is the related addition fact.

So, 8 − 5 = 3.

Jess has 8 ●●.

2️⃣ Jordan has 3 pencils.
Evan gives him some pencils.
Jordan now has 7 pencils.
How many pencils does Evan give Jordan?

I can use subtraction facts to solve addition sentences.

$3 +$ _____?_____ $= 7$
$7 - 3 = 4$ is the related subtraction fact.
So, $3 + 4 = 7$.
Evan gives Jordan 4 pencils.

TRY **Practice using related facts to solve problems**

Fill in each blank.

1️⃣ David has some fruit bars.
He gives 4 to his brother.
David has 5 bars left.
How many fruit bars does David have at first?

_____?_____ $- 4 = 5$

$4 + 5 =$ _____ is a related addition fact.

So, _____ $- 4 = 5$.

David has _____ fruit bars at first.

2 Kylie has 6 ladybugs in a jar.
She finds more ladybugs in a garden.
She now has 10 ladybugs.
How many ladybugs does Kylie find?

$$6 + \underline{}^{?} = 10$$

$10 - 6 = \underline{}$ is a related subtraction fact.

So, $6 + \underline{} = 10$.

Kylie finds $\underline{}$ ladybugs.

Fill in each blank.
Use related facts to help you.

3 $\underline{} - 4 = 4$

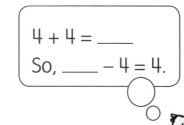

$4 + 4 = \underline{}$
So, $\underline{} - 4 = 4$.

4 $2 + \underline{} = 7$

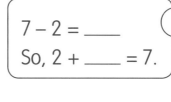

$7 - 2 = \underline{}$
So, $2 + \underline{} = 7$.

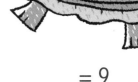

5 $\underline{} - 6 = 3$

6 $6 + \underline{} = 9$

7 $\underline{} + 3 = 5$

8 $10 - \underline{} = 6$

ENGAGE

1 Hannah says this number sentence is true.

   7 − 4 = 3

   Use two ways to tell your partner why Hannah is right.

2 Jack says this number sentence is false.

   9 − 3 = 5

   Use two ways to tell your partner why Jack is right.

LEARN Tell if a number sentence is true or false

1

   You can say 7 + 2 = 9 and 9 − 2 = 7.
   These number sentences are true.

   Can you say 7 + 2 = 8? No.
   What about 9 − 2 = 5? No.
   So, these sentences are false.

2 7 + 2 = 9   2 + 7 = 9
   Both number sentences have the same parts and whole.
   So, 7 + 2 = 2 + 7.
   This number sentence is true.

3 Is 7 + 2 = 4 + 3 a true number sentence?

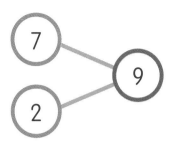

7 + 2 = 9

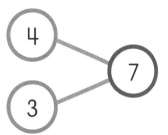

4 + 3 = 7

No, the number sentences do not have the same whole.
9 is not equal to 7.
So, this number sentence is false.

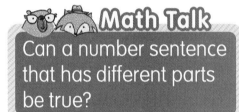

Can a number sentence that has different parts be true?

TRY Practice telling if a number sentence is true or false

Fill in each blank.

1 Is 5 + 3 = 9 a true number sentence?

5 + 3 = _____

Is _____ the same as 9? _____

So, this number sentence is _____ (true / false).

2 Is 4 = 10 − 6 a true number sentence?

10 − 6 = _____

Is _____ the same as 4? _____

So, this number sentence is _____ (true / false).

Use  or to help you.

1 Find three numbers that make 9.

2 Show two more ways to do this.

3 Find three numbers that make 10.
Show two ways to do this.

| 2 | 3 | 6 | 8 | 9 | 10 | + | − | = |

4 Use the cards above to make number sentences.
Use each card once in each number sentence.
Write all the number sentences you make.

Name: _____ Date: _____

INDEPENDENT PRACTICE

Make a fact family for each picture.

1

_____ + _____ = _____   _____ − _____ = _____

_____ + _____ = _____   _____ − _____ = _____

2

_____ + _____ = _____   _____ − _____ = _____

_____ + _____ = _____   _____ − _____ = _____

3

_____ + _____ = _____   _____ − _____ = _____

_____ + _____ = _____   _____ − _____ = _____

Solve.
Use related facts to help you.

4 Ian has some mangoes.
He gives 5 mangoes to Camilla.
Ian has 4 mangoes now.
How many mangoes does Ian have at first?

$$\underline{\hspace{3cm}}^{?} - 5 = 4$$

$4 + 5 = \underline{\hspace{3cm}}$ is the related addition fact.

So, $\underline{\hspace{3cm}} - 5 = 4$.

Ian has $\underline{\hspace{3cm}}$ mangoes at first.

5 Melanie has 7 toy cars.
Aki gives her some toy cars.
Melanie has 10 toy cars now.
How many toy cars does Aki give her?

$$7 + \underline{\hspace{3cm}}^{?} = 10$$

$10 - 7 = \underline{\hspace{3cm}}$ is the related subtraction fact.

So, $7 + \underline{\hspace{3cm}} = 10$.

Aki gives her $\underline{\hspace{3cm}}$ toy cars.

Fill in each blank.
Use related facts to help you.

6 _____ – 4 = 1

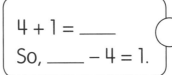
4 + 1 = ____
So, ____ – 4 = 1.

7 2 + _____ = 8

8 – 2 = ____
So, 2 + ____ = 8.

8 10 – _____ = 3

9 _____ + 5 = 10

Fill in each blank.

10 Is 10 = 7 + 3 a true number sentence?

7 + 3 = _____

Is your answer the same as 10? _____ (Yes / No)

So, this number sentence is _____ (true / false).

11 Is $4 = 8 - 6$ a true number sentence?

$8 - 6 = $ _____

Is your answer the same as 4? _____ (Yes / No)

So, this number sentence is _____ (true / false).

Is the number sentence true or false?
Circle the correct answer.

12 $8 + 4 = 4$ true   false

13 $9 - 5 = 4$ true   false

14 $4 = 7 - 2$ true   false

15 $6 = 3 + 3$ true   false

16 $8 + 0 = 4 + 4$ true   false

17 $2 + 5 = 8 - 1$ true   false

Mathematical Habit 3 Construct viable arguments

Are these sentences true or false?
Write down your thinking.

a   5 + 2 = 2 + 5

b   9 + 0 is greater than 0 + 9.

Problem Solving with Heuristics

1 **Mathematical Habit 1** Persevere in solving problems

Make two addition sentences with these numbers.
Use each number only once.

| 1 | 2 | 3 | 4 | 5 | 7 |

_____ + _____ = _____

_____ + _____ = _____

2 **Mathematical Habit 1** Persevere in solving problems

Make four subtraction sentences.

_____ − _____ = 3

_____ − _____ = 3

_____ − _____ = 3

_____ − _____ = 3

CHAPTER WRAP-UP

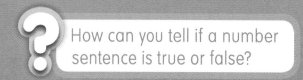

? How can you tell if a number sentence is true or false?

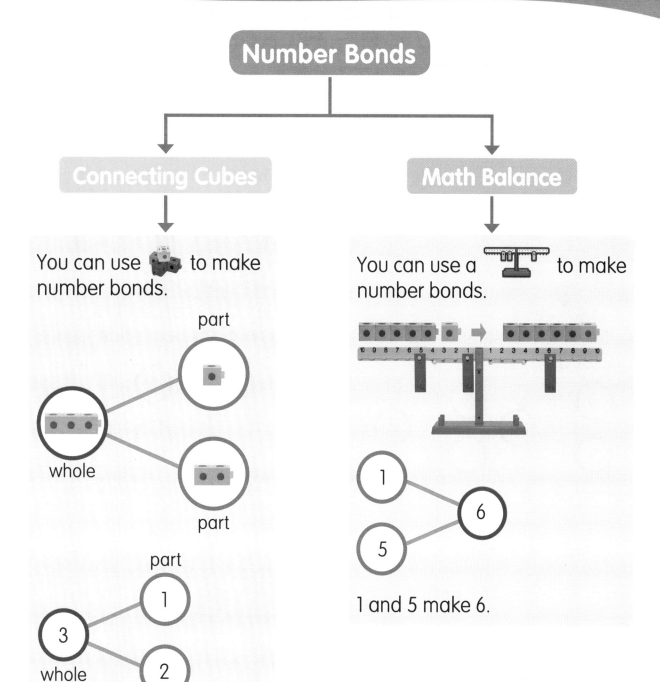

Number Bonds

Connecting Cubes

You can use [cubes] to make number bonds.

part

whole

part

part

3 whole

1 part

2 part

1 and 2 make 3.
1, 2, and 3 make a number bond.

Math Balance

You can use a [balance] to make number bonds.

1

5

6

1 and 5 make 6.

© 2020 Marshall Cavendish Education Pte Ltd

Addition Within 10

Ways to Add

You can count on from the greater number to add.

$3 + 2 = ?$

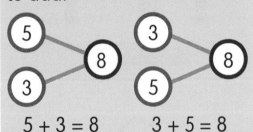

| 1 | 2 | **3** | 4 | 5 |

So, $3 + 2 = 5$.

You can use number bonds to add.

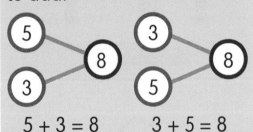

$5 + 3 = 8$ $3 + 5 = 8$

$5 + 3 = 3 + 5$

You can add in any order.

Solving Real-World Problems

You can solve real-world problems.

Julia has 6 pears.
Alex gives her 2 pears.
How many pears does Julia have now?

$6 + 2 = 8$

Julia has 8 pears now.

Making Addition Stories

You can tell addition stories about a picture.
Then, write an addition sentence for each story.

There is 1 yellow bean.
There are 2 green beans.

$1 + 2 = 3$

There are 3 beans in all.

Subtraction Within 10

Ways to Subtract

You can count on from the number that is less to subtract.

5 − 3 = ?

| 1 | 2 | **3** | 4 | 5 | 6 |

So, 5 − 3 = 2.

You can also count back from the greater number to subtract.

9 − 3 = ?

| 5 | 6 | 7 | 8 | **9** |

So, 9 − 3 = 6.

You can use number bonds to help you subtract.

9 − 8 = ?

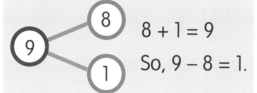

8 + 1 = 9

So, 9 − 8 = 1.

Solving Real-World Problems

You can solve real-world problems.
There are 4 eggs.
Lucy eats 1 egg.
How many eggs are left?

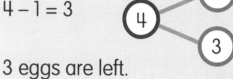

4 − 1 = 3

3 eggs are left.

Making Subtraction Stories

You can tell subtraction stories about a picture. Then, write a subtraction sentence for each story.

There are 3 lemons.
1 is green.
3 − 1 = 2
2 lemons are yellow.

Fact Family

Making a Fact Family

You can make a fact family.

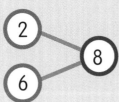

2 + 6 = 8   8 – 6 = 2
6 + 2 = 8   8 – 2 = 6

Each fact in a fact family has the same parts and whole.

True or False

You can check if a number sentence is true or false.
5 + 3 = 8 is true.
5 + 3 = 6 + 2 is true.

7 – 3 = 5 is false.
7 – 2 = 6 – 2 is false.

Using Related Facts to Solve Problems

You can use related addition facts to solve subtraction sentences.

$\underset{?}{\underline{}} - 4 = 2$

4 + 2 = 6 is the related addition fact.
So, 6 – 4 = 2.

You can use related subtraction facts to solve addition sentences.
1 + _____ = 3
3 – 1 = 2 is the related subtraction fact.
So, 1 + 2 = 3.

Name: _____ Date: _____

Complete each number bond.

1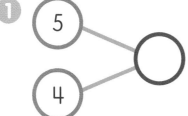

2

3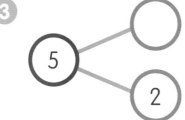

4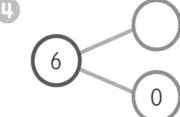

Add.
Use the number bond to help you.

5 How many goats are there in all?

_____ + _____ = _____ or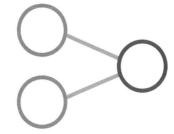

_____ + _____ = _____

There are _____ goats in all.

Add.
Count on from the greater number.

6

4

$4 + 3 = $ _____

7 $6 + 4 = $ _____

| 4 | 5 | 6 | 7 | 8 | 9 | 10 |

Make an addition story.
Fill in each blank.

8

_____ camels are eating.

_____ camels are drinking.

_____ ◯ _____ = _____

There are _____ camels in all.

Solve.

9 Jasmine has 4 baseballs.
She also has 1 volleyball.
How many balls does Jasmine have in all?

_____ ◯ _____ = _____

Jasmine has _____ balls in all.

Cross out to subtract.

10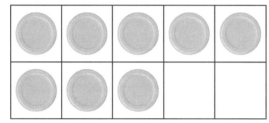

8 – 2 = _____

Subtract.
Count on from the number that is less.

| 1 | 2 | 3 | 4 | 5 | 6 | 7 | 8 | 9 | 10 |

11 9 – 6 = _____   **12** 10 – 5 = _____

Subtract.
Count back from the greater number.

| 1 | 2 | 3 | 4 | 5 | 6 | 7 | 8 | 9 | 10 |

13 8 – 1 = _____   **14** 9 – 4 = _____

Subtract.
Fill in each blank.

15 8 − 3 = ?

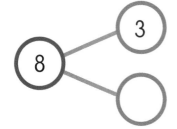

3 + _____ = 8

So, 8 − 3 = _____.

16 10 − 6 = ?

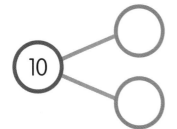

6 + _____ = 10

So, 10 − _____ = _____.

Make a subtraction story.
Fill in each blank.

17

cocoon

There are _____ cocoons.

_____ butterflies hatched from the cocoons.

_____ ◯ _____ = _____

There are _____ cocoons left.

Solve.

18 Ryan has 8 pieces of paper.
He folds 6 of them into cranes.
How many pieces of paper are not folded?

_____ ◯ _____ = _____

_____ pieces of paper are not folded.

Make a fact family for this picture.

19

_____ + _____ = _____   _____ − _____ = _____

_____ + _____ = _____   _____ − _____ = _____

Find each missing number.
Use related facts to help you.

20 $5 + \underline{\hspace{2cm}} = 7$

21 $8 = \underline{\hspace{2cm}} - 0$

22 $5 + 4 = \underline{\hspace{2cm}} + 6$

23 $2 + 4 = \underline{\hspace{2cm}} + 1$

Assessment Prep
Answer each question.

24

Color all the number sentences that tell the story.

| $10 - 3 = 7$ | $4 + 3 = 7$ | $7 - 3 = 4$ | $2 + 4 = 6$ |

25 Which number sentence is true?

    Ⓐ $8 + 2 = 6$ Ⓑ $6 = 4 + 3$

    Ⓒ $4 + 1 = 5$ Ⓓ $4 + 5 = 1$

Name: _____ Date: _____

School Bus Rides

1 Look at the picture.
Make 10 in three different ways.

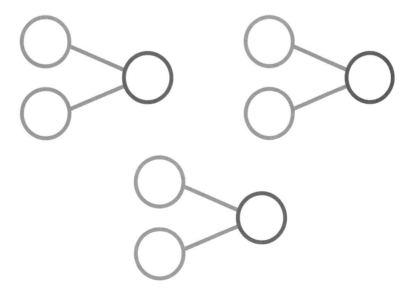

2 How many students are there in all?

_____ + _____ = _____

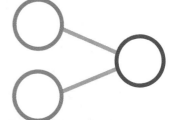

There are _____ students in all.

3 How many students are left on the bus?

_____ – _____ = _____

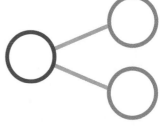

_____ students are left on the bus.

4 Look at the picture on Luke's book.
Write a fact family to match the picture.

_____ + _____ = _____   _____ − _____ = _____

_____ + _____ = _____   _____ − _____ = _____

5 Who is right?
Circle the name.

Andre   Mai

1 + 4 = _____   10 − 5 = _____

Andre   /   Mai   is right.

Rubric

Point(s)	Level	My Performance
7–8	4	• Most of my answers are correct. • I show all my work correctly. • I explain my thinking clearly and completely.
5–6.5	3	• Some of my answers are correct. • I show some of my work correctly. • I explain my thinking clearly.
3–4.5	2	• A few of my answers are correct. • I show little work correctly. • I explain some of my thinking clearly.
0–2.5	1	• A few of my answers are correct. • I show little or no work. • I do not explain my thinking clearly.

Teacher's Comments

Chapter 3
Shapes and Patterns

Each side of a cube is a square.

What shapes do you see around you?
How can you tell them apart?

Name: _____   Date: _____

Recognizing shapes

These are shapes.

square

rectangle

circle

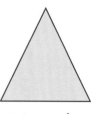
triangle

These are also shapes.

cube

cylinder

sphere

cone

Name: _____   Date: _____

1 Exploring Flat Shapes

Learning Objectives:
- Identify, classify, and describe flat shapes.
- Divide flat shapes into two and four equal parts, and describe the parts.
- Describe the whole flat shape as a sum of its parts.

New Vocabulary
trapezoid
alike
different
divide
half of
halves
half-circle
quarter of
quarters
quarter-circle
fourth of
fourths

THINK

Fold a square into two equal parts.
What shapes do you get?
How many ways can you do it?
Next, fold the square into four equal parts.
What shapes do you get?
How many ways can you do it?
Talk about how you fold the square with your partner.

ENGAGE

Take some .
Turn each shape around.
Which shapes look different when you turn them?
Which shape always looks the same?
Talk about your answers with your partner.

Recognize flat shapes

①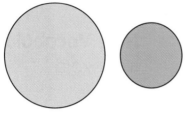

circles   triangles

squares   rectangles

②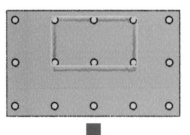

> This is a geoboard.
> Let us make a rectangle on it.

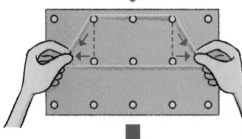

> Stretch the ends of the rectangle the way you see on the geoboard.

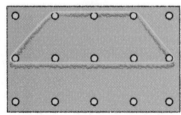

> You get a new shape.
> This shape is called a trapezoid.

Hands-on Activity Identifying sides and corners in flat shapes

Work in pairs.

Take some ◼◻⬣▲.

① **Mathematical Habit 7** Make use of structure

Call out, "a shape with four sides."
Ask your partner to show you any shape with four sides.

② Trade places and repeat ①.
Call out:

  a   a shape with three sides

  b   a shape with no sides

  c   a shape with two sides

③ **Mathematical Habit 7** Make use of structure

Call out, "a shape with four corners."
Ask your partner to show you any shape with four corners.

④ Trade places and repeat ③.
Call out:

  a   a shape with three corners

  b   a shape with no corners

  c   a shape with two corners

TRY Practice identifying sides and corners in flat shapes

Trace each shape.
Count the number of sides and corners.
Then, write the number.

1 square

_____ sides

_____ corners

2 triangle

_____ sides

_____ corners

3 rectangle

_____ sides

_____ corners

4 trapezoid

_____ sides

_____ corners

Math Talk
Are squares and rectangles the same?
Share your thinking with your partner.

ENGAGE

Take some  and some colored paper.
Trace and cut out each shape.
Sort your shapes in different ways.
Talk about how you sorted your shapes with your partner.

LEARN Sort shapes in different ways

1

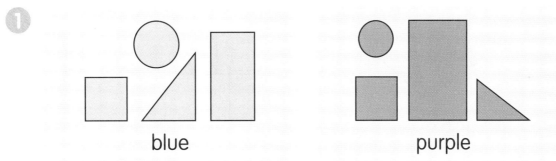

blue   purple

These shapes are sorted by color.
They are alike.

2

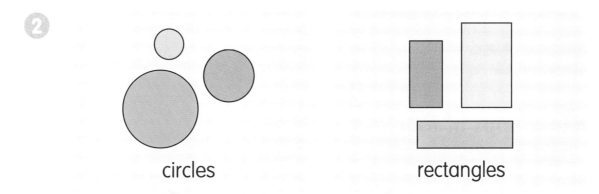

circles   rectangles

These shapes are sorted by shape.

3

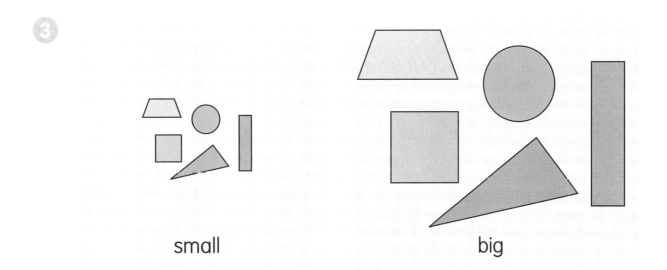

small   big

These shapes are sorted by size.

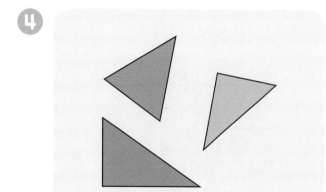

3 sides and 3 corners

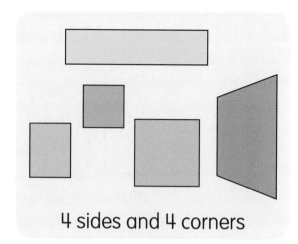

4 sides and 4 corners

These shapes are sorted by the number of sides and corners.

Hands-on Activity Telling how shapes are alike and different

Work in groups of four.
Your teacher will give you a set of shapes.

① Choose a shape.

② **Mathematical Habit 7** Make use of structure

Share your shapes.
Talk about how your shapes are alike or different.

③ Repeat ① and ② a few more times.

④ Work together to sort all the shapes in different ways.
Talk about the different ways you sort your shapes.

TRY Practice sorting shapes in different ways

Answer each question.

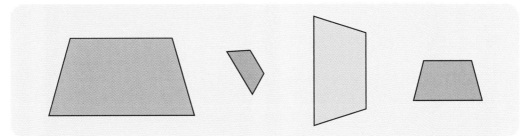

1 How are these shapes alike? _____

2 How are they different? _____

Circle the shapes that are of the same size and shape.

3

**Draw and color any three shapes.
Then, answer each question.**

4 How are your shapes alike? _____

5 How are they different? _____

ENGAGE

1. Fold a square once to make two equal parts.
   Fold the square again to make another two equal parts.
   How many equal parts do you get in all?

2. How can you fold a triangle with equal sides to make
   a   three equal parts,   b   four equal parts?

LEARN Divide shapes into equal parts

1

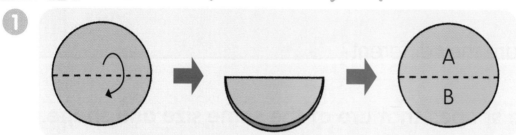

The circle is folded into two equal parts, A and B.
Each part is one **half** of the circle.

> Two equal parts, or two halves, make one whole.

One half of a circle is called a **half-circle**.

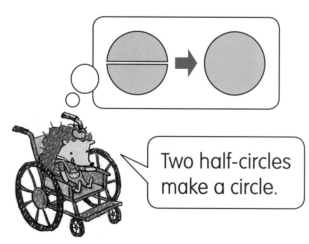

> Two half-circles make a circle.

2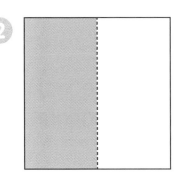

The square is divided into two equal parts.
Each part is one half of the square.
Each part is smaller than the square.

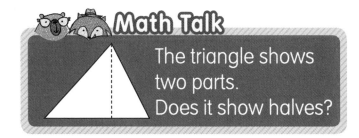

Math Talk

The triangle shows two parts.
Does it show halves?

3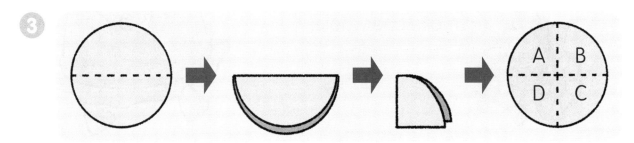

The circle is folded into four equal parts, A, B, C, and D.
Each part is one **quarter** of the circle.

Four quarters make one whole.

One quarter of a circle is called a **quarter-circle**.

Four quarter-circles make a circle.

4

The square is divided into four equal parts. Each part is one fourth of the square.

One fourth has the same meaning as one quarter.

Four fourths make one whole.

5 Which square has smaller parts?

 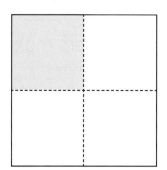

You get smaller parts each time you divide a shape into more equal parts.

Math Talk

Is a half-circle or a quarter-circle smaller? How can you tell?

Activity 1   Folding and dividing shapes into two parts

① Your teacher will give you these shapes.

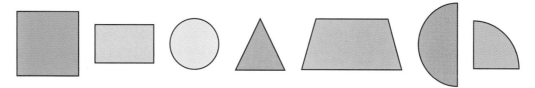

Fold and cut each shape to show halves.

② **Mathematical Habit 3** Construct viable arguments

Talk about why the halves are equal with your partner.

> Do both of you fold each shape the same way?
> Are there different ways to do it?

③ Your teacher will give you these shapes.

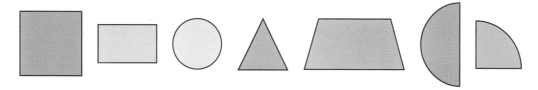

Fold and cut each shape so that the parts are not equal.

④ **Mathematical Habit 3** Construct viable arguments

Talk about why the parts are not equal with your partner.

Activity 2   Folding and dividing shapes into quarters

① Your teacher will give you these shapes.

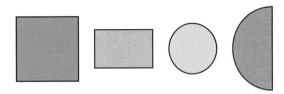

Fold and cut each shape to show quarters.

② **Mathematical Habit** 3 **Construct viable arguments**
Talk about why the quarters are equal with your partner.

TRY Practice identifying halves and quarters

Color the shapes that show halves.
Fold shapes to help you.

   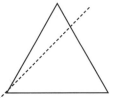 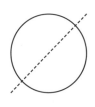

Color the shapes that show quarters.
Fold shapes to help you.

②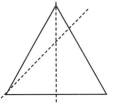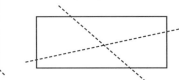

Exploring Solid Shapes

Learning Objective:
- Identify, classify, and sort solid shapes.

New Vocabulary
rectangular prism
pyramid

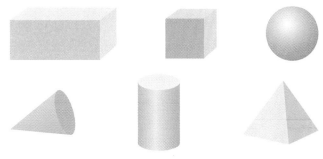

Name these solid shapes.
Which shapes can you stack?
Which shapes can you stack but **not** slide?
How do you know?

ENGAGE

Name two solid shapes that are different.
How are they different?
Name two solid shapes which are alike in at least three ways.
How are they alike?

LEARN Recognize solid shapes

1 Use your finger to trace these solid shapes.
Talk about the shapes as a class.

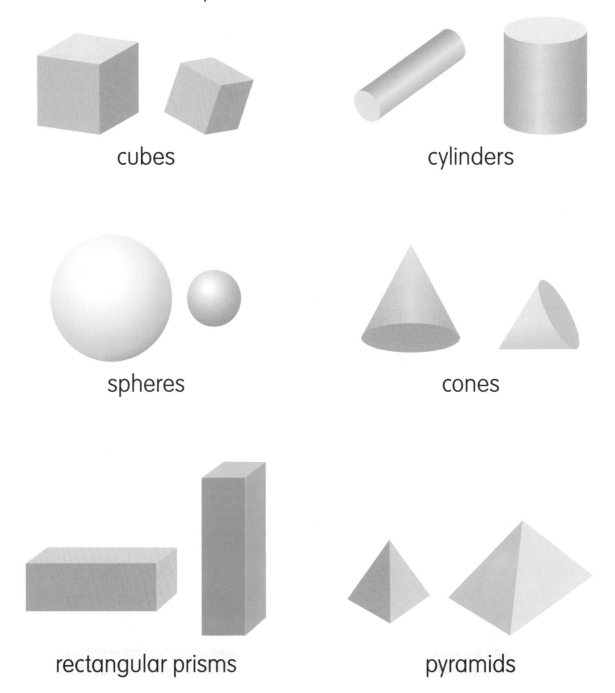

cubes

cylinders

spheres

cones

rectangular prisms

pyramids

Hands-on Activity Identifying different solid shapes

Work in groups of three.

Take some 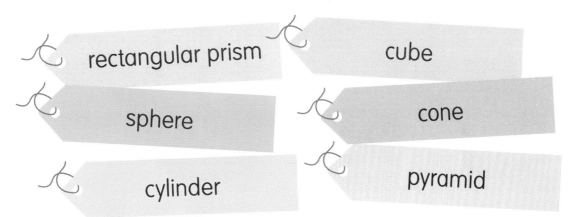.

① Call out the name of a solid shape.

rectangular prism	cube
sphere	cone
cylinder	pyramid

② Ask your group to show the correct solid shapes.

③ Trade places.
Repeat ① and ②.
Continue the activity until you have called all the solid shapes.

Cube.

Practice recognizing and identifying solid shapes

Circle the cubes.

1

Name each solid shape.

2

_____

3

_____

4

_____

5

_____

ENGAGE

Take some .
Roll, slide, and stack the solid shapes.
Talk about how you move the shapes with your partner.

LEARN Move solid shapes in different ways

① You can stack and slide these shapes.

② You can roll these shapes.

Hands-on Activity 〉 Moving solid shapes

Take some .

① Find out which shapes you can stack, slide, or roll.
Make an ✗ in your table to show what you find.

Solid Shape	Stack	Roll	Slide
Rectangular Prism			
Sphere			
Cube			
Cylinder			
Cone			
Pyramid			

② **Mathematical Habit** 7 **Make use of structure**

Talk about the answers to these questions with your partner.

a   Which shapes can you stack?

b   Which shapes can you roll?

c   Which shapes can you not slide?

d   Which two shapes can be moved in the same ways?

e   Is there a shape that you can stack, roll, and slide?

TRY Practice recognizing how solid shapes move

Sort the solid shapes.

1 Circle the shapes that can stack.

2 Circle the shapes that can roll.

3 Circle the shapes that can slide.

Write the names of the solid shapes.

4 Which solid shape can stack and roll? _____

5 Which solid shapes can stack and slide?

_____, _____, _____

6 Which solid shapes can roll and slide?

_____, _____

7 Which solid shape can stack, roll, and slide? _____

GUESS THE SHAPES!

It has 3 sides and 3 corners.

It is a triangle.

What you need:

Players: 2

Materials: , , An empty bag

What to do:

Put all the and in a bag.

1. Player 1 takes a shape from the bag and hides it. Then, he or she describes it.

2. Player 2 guesses the name of the shape. Each correct answer receives one point.

3. Trade places. Repeat 1 and 2.

Who is the winner?

The player with more points after five rounds wins.

INDEPENDENT PRACTICE

Name each solid shape.

_____

_____

Circle the rectangular prisms.

Color the cylinders red.
Color the pyramids blue.

 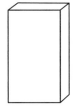 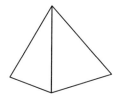

Read each clue.
Then, write the names of the solid shapes.

5 You can stack and slide it. _____, _____,

_____

6 You can only roll it. _____

7 You can roll and slide it. _____, _____

8 You can stack, slide, and roll it. _____

Answer each question.

9

There is one way you can move all of these shapes.
What is it?

_____

10 Amy places some solid shapes at the top of a slope.

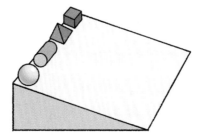

Which two shapes will roll down the slope?

_____

3 Using Shapes to Make Pictures and Models

Learning Objectives:
- Compose flat shapes to create a picture or a new shape.
- Identify flat shapes in a picture.
- Compose solid shapes to create a model.
- Identify solid shapes in a model.

THINK

The following shows the shape of a model when you look at it from the side.

Use to build the model.

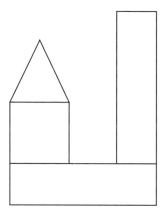

ENGAGE

Use these four squares to make a bigger square.

How many rectangles can you find in your new square?

LEARN Use flat shapes to make pictures

1 You can use flat shapes to make pictures.

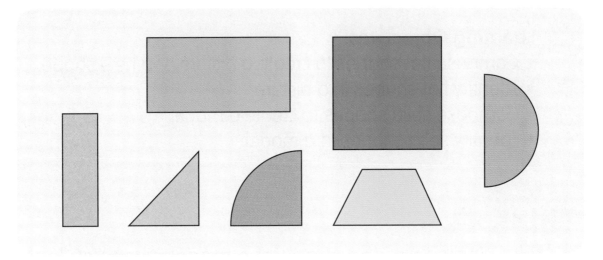

What shapes do you see?

I can make a picture like this.

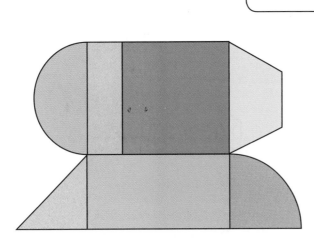

I can make a picture like this.

2 You can name the shapes in a picture.

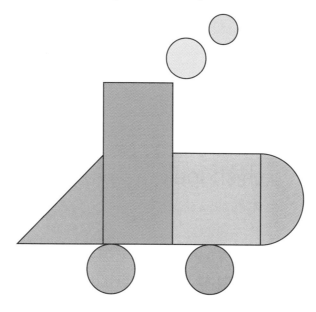

Type of Shapes	Number
Triangle	1
Rectangle	1
Square	1
Circle	4
Half-Circle	1

Hands-on Activity

Activity 1 Using flat shapes to make pictures

① Use these shapes to make a picture.

You can use some or all of the shapes.

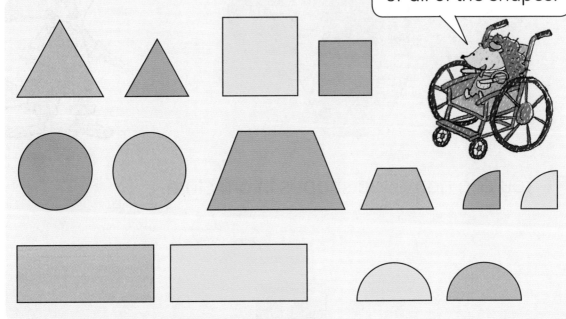

② How many of each shape do you use?

Activity 2 Using cut-outs to make shapes

Your teacher will give you a set of shapes.

① Put two shapes together to make each of these shapes.

 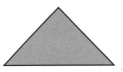

© 2020 Marshall Cavendish Education Pte Ltd

Activity 3 Using 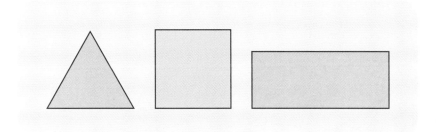 to make bigger shapes

① **Mathematical Habit 1** Persevere in solving problems

Use ▰◐▲ to make each of these shapes.

② How many ways can you do it?
Share how you do it with your partner.

Activity 4 Making new shapes

Take some 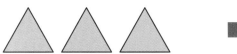.

① **Mathematical Habit 1** Persevere in solving problems

Put any of the shapes together to make a new shape.

② **Mathematical Habit 1** Persevere in solving problems

Use the new shape to make another new shape.

Example:

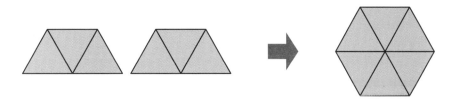

TRY Practice identifying flat shapes in pictures

Count the flat shapes in the picture.
Then, write the number.

1 This picture is made of many flat shapes.

How many of these shapes can you find?

Type of Shapes	Number
Triangle	
Rectangle	
Square	
Circle	
Half-Circle	
Trapezoid	

Draw lines to make shapes.
Make the number of each shape in the table.

2

Type of Shapes	Number
Triangle	2
Trapezoid	1
Quarter-Circle	2

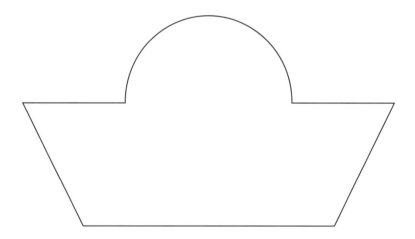

ENGAGE

Use to make these models.

What shapes do you use?
What shapes do you see from the top?
What shapes do you see from the side?
Draw them.
Then, talk about your answers with your partner.

LEARN Use solid shapes to make models

1 You can use solid shapes to make models.

What shapes do you see?

I can make a model like this.

I can make a model like this.

2 You can name the solid shapes in a model.

Type of Shapes	Number
Rectangular Prism	2
Cylinder	2
Sphere	1
Cone	1

Math Talk

How many cubes and pyramids do you see in the model?

Hands-on Activity Using solid shapes to make models

① Use 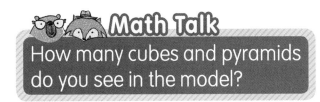 to make your own model.

② Count how many of each shape you used.

Type of Shapes	Number
Cube	
Sphere	
Pyramid	
Cylinder	
Cone	
Rectangular Prism	

Count the solid shapes in the model.
Then, write the number.

1

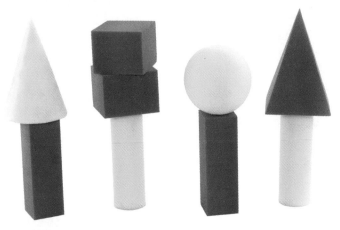

How many of these shapes can you find?

Type of Shapes	Number
Cube	
Sphere	
Pyramid	
Cylinder	
Cone	
Rectangular Prism	

INDEPENDENT PRACTICE

Count the flat shapes in the picture.
Then, write the number.

 1

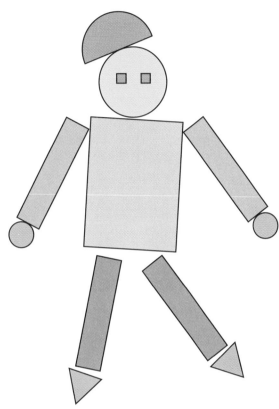

Type of Shapes	Number
Triangle	
Rectangle	
Square	
Circle	
Half-Circle	
Quarter-Circle	

Look at the shape on the left.
Then, circle two shapes that make that shape.

2

3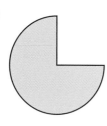

Draw a line to make two new shapes.
Then, write the names of the shapes you make.

4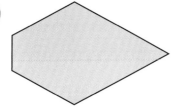

_____ , _____

Draw lines to make these shapes.

5

Type of Shapes	Number
Half-Circle	1
Rectangle	1
Trapezoid	1
Quarter-Circle	2

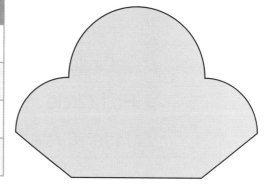

Circle all the possible models.

6 Tyler uses a cone, a cube, and a rectangular prism to make a model.

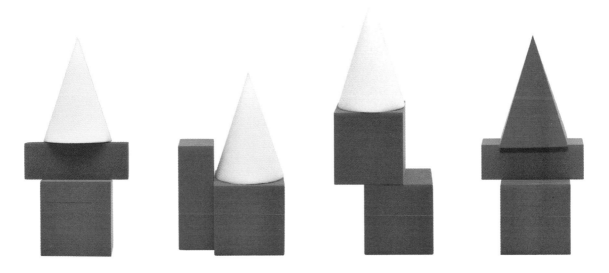

Count the solid shapes in the model. Then, write the number.

7

Type of Shapes	Number
Cube	
Sphere	
Rectangular Prism	
Pyramid	
Cylinder	
Cone	

8

Type of Shapes	Number
Cube	
Sphere	
Rectangular Prism	
Pyramid	
Cylinder	
Cone	

Write the name and number of each solid shape in the model.

9

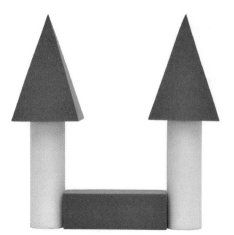

Seeing Shapes Around Us

Learning Objective:
• Identify flat and solid shapes in real life.

 **THINK**

This is a traffic cone.
What shapes do you see from the top?
What shapes do you see from the side?
Draw them.

ENGAGE

Look around you.

1 Tell your partner two objects that have each of these shapes.

a   b   c

2 Each picture shows how two different objects look like from the top or side.
What can the two objects be for each picture?
Share your answers with your partner.

a 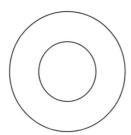   b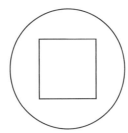

LEARN Identify flat shapes around you

1
This is a book.
It has the shape of a rectangle.

2
This is a clock.
It has the shape of a circle.

3
This is a sandwich.
It has the shape of a triangle.

Hands-on Activity Tracing the bottoms of objects

Work in groups of three.
Your teacher will give you some objects.

1 Take an object.
Trace the bottom of each object.
Write the name of the shape you get.

2 Repeat 1 for the rest of the objects.

Object	Shape

TRY Practice identifying flat shapes around you

Look at the picture.
Name the shape you see.

1 This is a slice of cheese.

It has the shape of a _____.

Trace the bottom of each object.
Name the shape you get.

2

_____

3

_____

4

_____

5

_____

ENGAGE

1 Look at a cube from the top.
Draw the shape you see.

2 Find objects that show each of these pictures.

a   b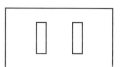

LEARN Identify solid shapes around you

①
This is a box.
It has the shape of a rectangular prism.

②
This is a tennis ball.
It has the shape of a sphere.

Hands-on Activity

Work in pairs.

Activity 1   Tracing each side of a solid shape

Take some .

① Trace the sides of each solid shape.
What flat shapes do you make?

a

_____

b

_____

c

_____

d

_____

Activity 2   Finding shapes around you

① Look around your school for objects of these shapes. Write the names in the table to show what you find.

Type of Shapes	Object 1	Object 2
Cylinder		
Rectangular Prism		
Cube		
Sphere		
Cone		
Pyramid		

② Find two objects that have these shapes on them.

Type of Shapes	Object 1	Object 2
Rectangle		
Circle		
Triangle		

TRY Practice identifying shapes around you

Look at the picture.
Then, answer each question.

1 This is a sponge.

What shape is it? _____

What flat shapes do you see? _____

Look at each picture.
Write the shapes you see.

2

_____ , _____

3

_____ , _____ ,

_____

4

_____ , _____ ,

_____ , _____

5

_____ , _____ ,

_____ , _____

INDEPENDENT PRACTICE

Name each shape.

This is a photo frame.

What flat shape do you see? _____

This is a number cube.

What solid shape do you see? _____

Look at each picture.
Answer each question.

3. This is a sharpener.

What shape is it? _____

What flat shapes do you see? _____

4. This is a book.

What shape is it? _____

What flat shapes do you see? _____

5 This is a connecting cube.

Name all the solid shapes you see. _____, _____

Name all the flat shapes you see. _____, _____

Look at the pictures.
Name the solid shapes you see.
Name the flat shapes you see.

6

Solid shapes _____, _____

Flat shapes _____, _____

7

Solid shapes _____, _____

Flat shape _____

Using Flat Shapes to Make Patterns

Learning Objective:
• Use flat shapes to identify, continue, and make patterns.

> **New Vocabulary**
> repeating pattern

 **THINK**

The pattern below is made up of numbers and shapes.

What comes next?

   ENGAGE

Use nine shapes to make a pattern.
Use only squares, triangles, and circles.
Share your pattern with your partner and talk about it.

LEARN Recognize repeating patterns involving flat shapes

1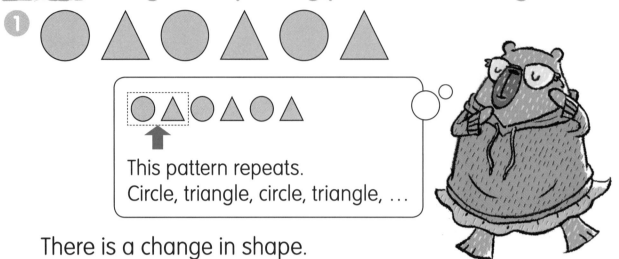

This pattern repeats.
Circle, triangle, circle, triangle, …

There is a change in shape.

2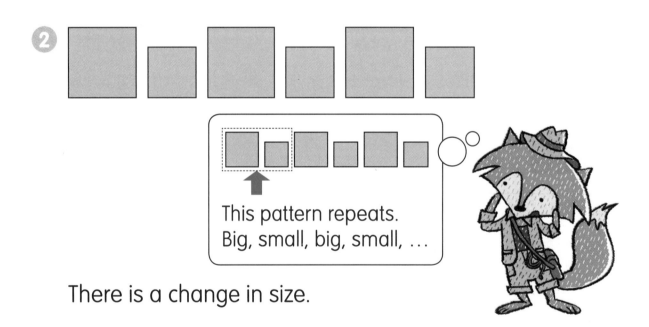

This pattern repeats.
Big, small, big, small, …

There is a change in size.

3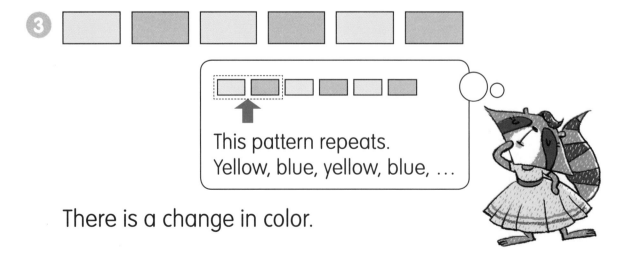

This pattern repeats.
Yellow, blue, yellow, blue, …

There is a change in color.

Hands-on Activity Using flat shapes to make patterns

Work in pairs.

Take some ⬛🔵🔺.

① **Mathematical Habit 8** Look for patterns

Make a repeating pattern with two shapes.

② Draw the pattern you have made.

③ **Mathematical Habit 8** Look for patterns

Ask another pair to draw what comes next.

④ **Mathematical Habit 8** Look for patterns

Use three shapes to make a pattern.

⑤ Repeat ② and ③.

TRY Practice finding missing shapes in a pattern

Circle the shape that comes next in each pattern.

1

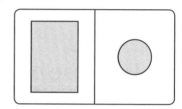

2

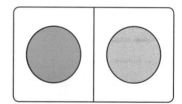

3

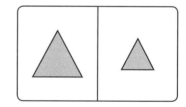

4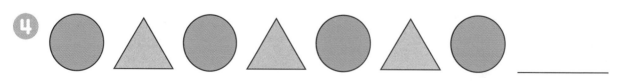

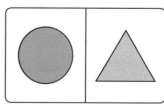

Name: _____ Date: _____

INDEPENDENT PRACTICE

Circle the missing shape in each pattern.

1

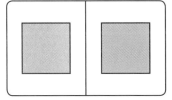

2

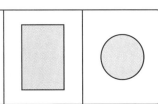

3

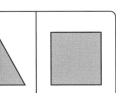

4

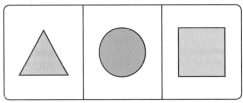

5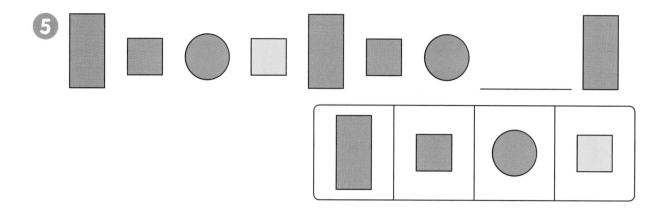

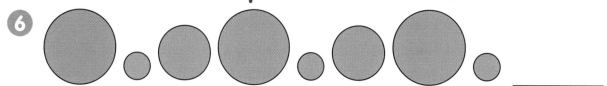

Draw and color the shape that comes next.

6

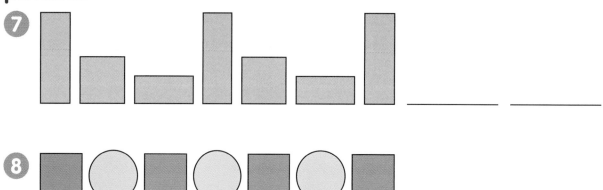

Draw and color the shapes that come next in each pattern.

7

8

Using Solid Shapes to Make Patterns

Learning Objective:
- Use solid shapes to identify, continue, and make patterns.

 THINK

The pattern below is made up of numbers and shapes.

, 13, , _____, , 9, , 7, , 5, _____, 3

What is missing to complete the pattern?

ENGAGE

Use nine solid shapes to make a pattern.
Use only cubes, rectangular prisms, and cones.
Share your pattern with your partner and talk about it.

LEARN Recognize repeating patterns involving solid shapes

1

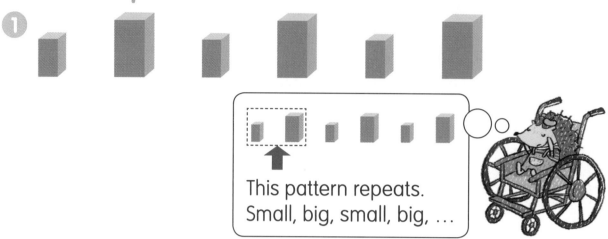

This pattern repeats.
Small, big, small, big, ...

There is a change in size.

2

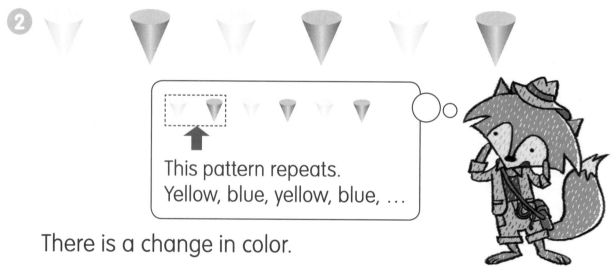

This pattern repeats.
Yellow, blue, yellow, blue, ...

There is a change in color.

3

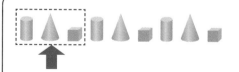

This pattern repeats.
Cylinder, cone, cube, cylinder, cone, cube, ...

There is a change in shape.

Hands-on Activity Using solid shapes to make patterns

Work in groups.

Take some 🔲△🔵.

① **Mathematical Habit** 8 **Look for patterns**

Use two different solid shapes to make a pattern.

② **Mathematical Habit** 8 **Look for patterns**

Ask your classmate to show what comes next.

③ **Mathematical Habit** 8 **Look for patterns**

Use three different solid shapes to make a pattern.

④ Repeat ②.

TRY Practice finding missing shapes in a pattern

Circle the shape that comes next in each pattern.

①   _____

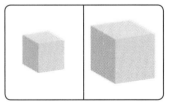

2  _____

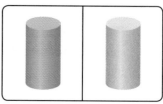

3  _____

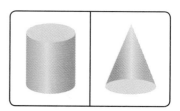

4  _____

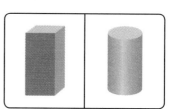

INDEPENDENT PRACTICE

Look at each pattern.
Circle the correct answer.

There is a change in   color   /   shape   /   size   .

 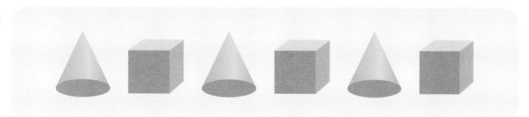

There is a change in   color   /   shape   /   size   .

 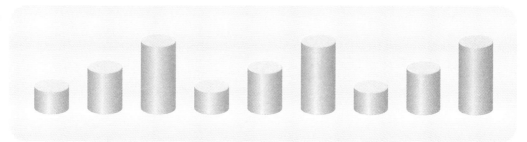

There is a change in   color   /   shape   /   size   .

 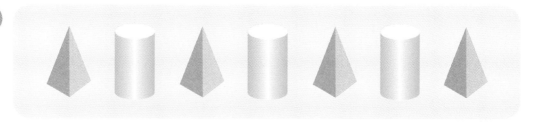

There is a change in   color   /   shape   /   size   .

Circle the missing shapes in each pattern.

5  _____ _____

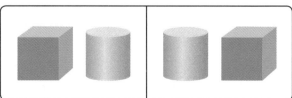

6

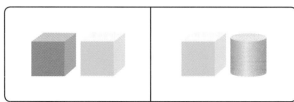

7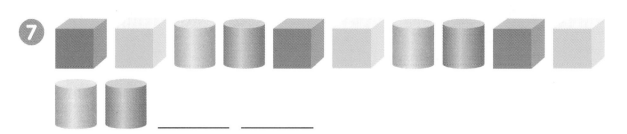

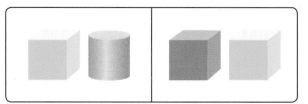

Mathematical Habit **1** Persevere in solving problems

Walk around your school.
What shapes do you see?
Write the names or draw the objects in the correct boxes below.

Triangle	Rectangle	Circle

Cylinder	Rectangular Prism	Cone

Problem Solving with Heuristics

1 **Mathematical Habit 7** Make use of structure

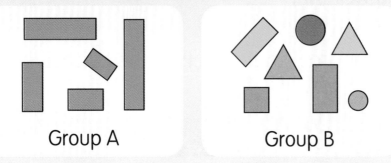

Group A   Group B

How are these shapes sorted?

2 **Mathematical Habit 3** Construct viable arguments

Matt says he has a shape with four sides.
Ana says the shape is a square.
Is she correct?

3 **Mathematical Habit 8** Look for patterns
Circle the shape that comes next.

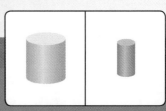

CHAPTER WRAP-UP

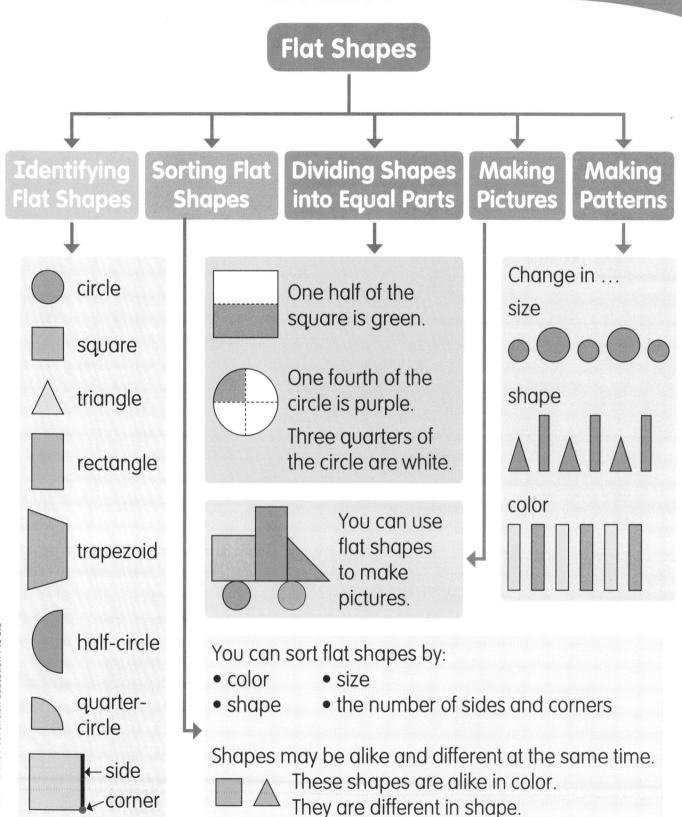

Flat Shapes

Identifying Flat Shapes

- circle
- square
- triangle
- rectangle
- trapezoid
- half-circle
- quarter-circle
- ← side
- ← corner

Sorting Flat Shapes

You can sort flat shapes by:
- color
- shape
- size
- the number of sides and corners

Shapes may be alike and different at the same time.
These shapes are alike in color.
They are different in shape.

Dividing Shapes into Equal Parts

One half of the square is green.

One fourth of the circle is purple.

Three quarters of the circle are white.

You can use flat shapes to make pictures.

Making Pictures

Making Patterns

Change in …
size

shape

color

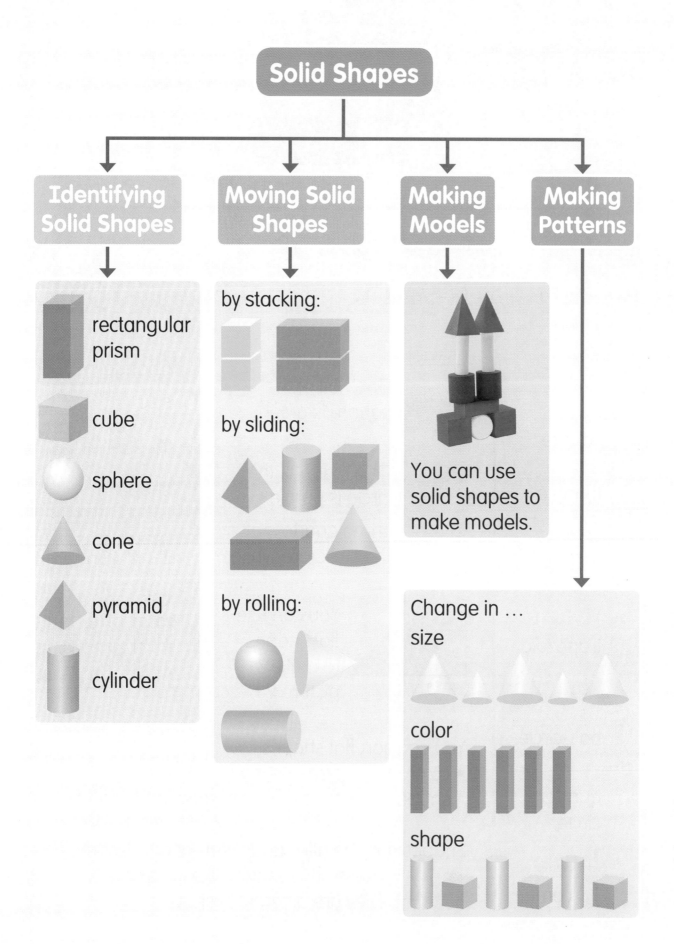

Solid Shapes

Identifying Solid Shapes

rectangular prism

cube

sphere

cone

pyramid

cylinder

Moving Solid Shapes

by stacking:

by sliding:

by rolling:

Making Models

You can use solid shapes to make models.

Making Patterns

Change in ...
size

color

shape

Name: _____ Date: _____

Using Modeling Clay to Make Shapes

1 Peyton makes these shapes from modeling clay.

   a   How are these shapes alike?

   b   How are these shapes different?

2 Brandon makes a trapezoid.

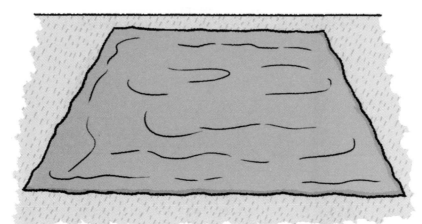

He draws the trapezoid he makes.

a How many corners does the trapezoid have? _____
Circle them in blue.

b How many sides does the trapezoid have? _____
Trace each side in red.

a What is the name of the shape? _____

b Can this shape stack, roll, or slide?
Color the boxes to show what the shape can do.

stack	roll	slide

4 Mariah makes this model of a table.
What shapes do you see?
Circle them.

circle   square   rectangle

cone   pyramid   cylinder

5 Owen draws the shape he sees from the top.

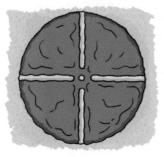

This is the shape that Owen draws.

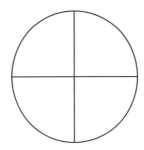

   a How many equal parts do you see? _____

   b What shape are these equal parts? _____

   c Color half of the circle red.

6 Angelia makes a pattern below.
What comes next in the pattern?
Circle.

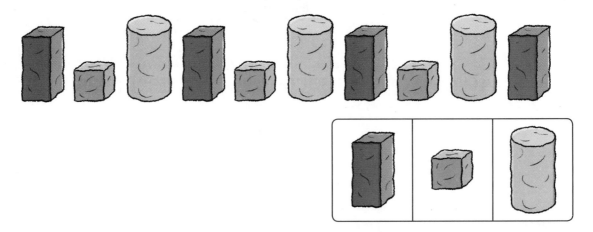

Rubric

Point(s)	Level	My Performance
7–8	4	• Most of my answers are correct. • I show all my work correctly. • I explain my thinking clearly and completely.
5–6.5	3	• Some of my answers are correct. • I show some of my work correctly. • I explain my thinking clearly.
3–4.5	2	• A few of my answers are correct. • I show little work correctly. • I explain some of my thinking clearly.
0–2.5	1	• A few of my answers are correct. • I show little or no work. • I do not explain my thinking clearly.

Teacher's Comments

STEAM

A Home in the Trees

Imagine your own tree house.
What would it look like?
What shapes would you use to build your own tree house?

Task

Design your own tree house.
Work in groups of four.

1. Visit the library to read about tree houses.
2. Collect some flat shapes.
3. Use these shapes to design your own tree house.
4. Write a story about your tree house.
5. Share your story with the class.

Are there enough apples for the squirrels?

How can you tell?

How can you order any three numbers from 1 to 20?

Name: _____ Date: _____

Counting

One, two, three, four, five, six, seven, eight, nine, ten.
There are ten frogs.

▶ Quick Check

Count.
Write each number and word.

1 How many chickens are there?

Number _____ Word _____

2 How many chicks are there?

Number _____ Word _____

Comparing numbers

····· 8

························· 5

There are more bananas than monkeys.
There are fewer monkeys than bananas.
8 is greater than 5.
5 is less than 8.

▶ **Quick Check**

Write each missing number.

································· _____

·· _____

3 _____ is greater than _____.

4 _____ is less than _____.

Number patterns

This is a pattern.

a

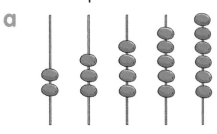

2   3   4   5   6

Each number is 1 more than the number before it.

b

5   4   3   2   1

Each number is 1 less than the number before it.

▶ **Quick Check**

How many flowers come next in the pattern? Draw them.

5

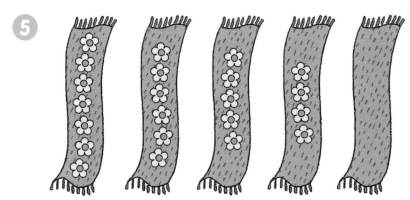

_____ flowers come next in the pattern.

Write each missing number in the number pattern.

6 _____, 5, 6, 7, 8, _____

Counting to 20

Learning Objectives:
- Count on from 10 to 20.
- Read and write 11 to 20 in numbers and words.

THINK

Karina sees some monkeys in a zoo.
The zookeeper tells her there are fewer than 15 monkeys.
Karina writes the addition sentence to show the number of monkeys.

10 + _____ = _____

Talk about all five answers with your partner.

ENGAGE

Use 🔵 and four ⬜.
a   Show 10.
    Then, show 3 more.
b   Now, show 8.
    Then, show 5 more.

What do you notice about the numbers formed in **a** and **b**?

LEARN Count on from 10

1 You can count on from 10.

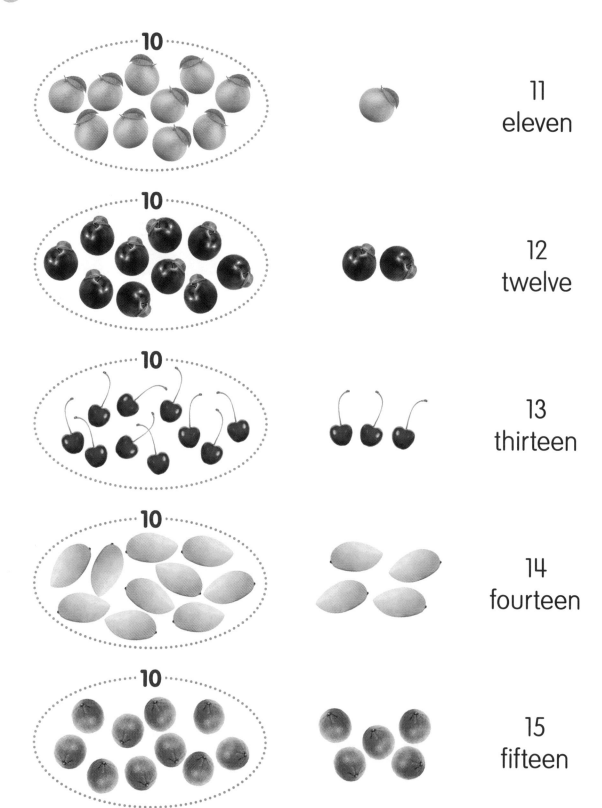

10   11 eleven

10   12 twelve

10   13 thirteen

10   14 fourteen

10   15 fifteen

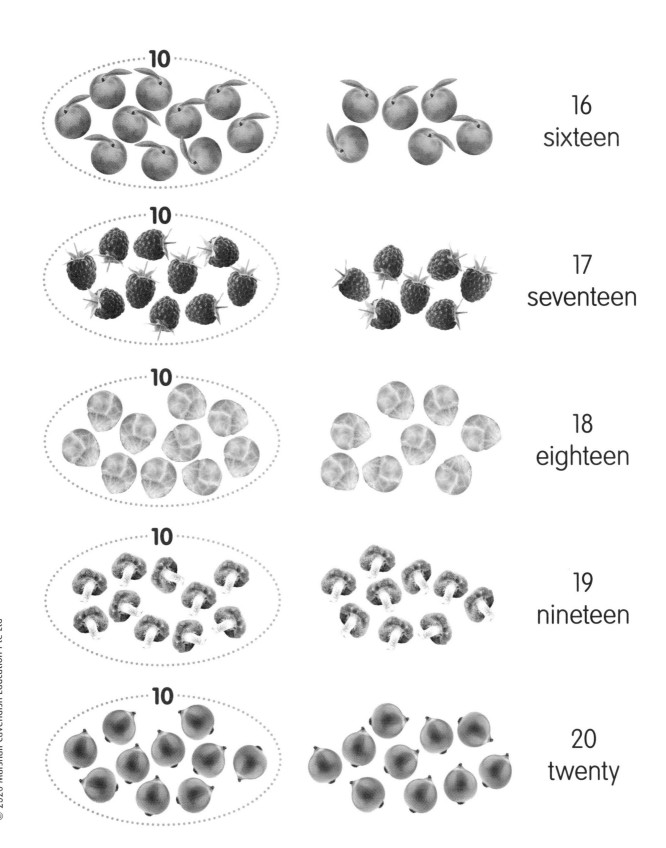

10   16
                          sixteen

10   17
                          seventeen

10   18
                          eighteen

10   19
                          nineteen

10   20
                          twenty

2 You can make a 10.
Then, count on.

10 and 3 make 13.   10 + 3 = 13

Hands-on Activity Counting on from 10

Work in pairs.

① Take some 🎲.

② Ask your partner to count the number of 🎲.
Ask him or her to make a 10 using ⊞⊞.
Then, put the remaining 🎲 on another ⊞⊞.

③ a Write the number. _____

   b Write the word. _____

④ Trade places.
Repeat ① to ③.

TRY Practice counting on from 10

Count on from 10.
Then, write the number and word.

①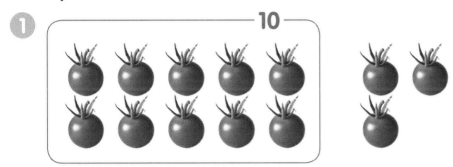

Number _____ Word _____

Make a 10.
Next, count on.
Then, fill in each blank.

②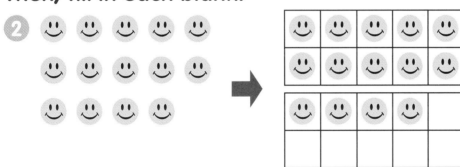

_____ and _____ make 14.

_____ + _____ = _____

Write each missing number.

③ 10 and 7 make _____.   10 + 7 = _____

④ 10 and 10 make _____.   10 + 10 = _____

MATCH UP!

It is a match!

16   sixteen

What you need:

Players: 2
Materials: Number cards, Word cards

What to do:

Place the cards face down on the table.

1️⃣ Player 1 turns over a number and a word card.
Keep the cards if they match.
Turn them back if they do not.

2️⃣ Trade places.
Repeat 1️⃣.
The game ends when all the cards are matched.

Who is the winner?

The player who collects more cards wins.

INDEPENDENT PRACTICE

Count on from 10.
Then, write each number.

 10

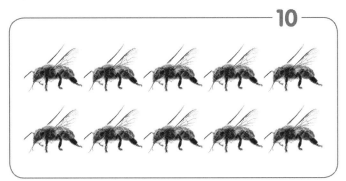

_____

 10

_____

_____

Make a 10.
Next, count on.
Then, write each number.

4

_____

5

_____

6

_____

Write each missing number.

 7

      10 and 2 make _____.

      $10 + 2 =$ _____

8

      10 and 5 make _____.

      $10 + 5 =$ _____

9 10 and 1 make _____.

      $10 + 1 =$ _____

10 10 and 9 make _____.

      _____ + _____ = _____

Make a 10.
Next, count on.
Then, write each number and word.

11

Number _____ Word _____

12

Number _____ Word _____

13

Number _____ Word _____

2 Place Value

Learning Objectives:
- Use a place-value chart to show numbers to 20.
- Use tens and ones to show numbers to 20.

New Vocabulary
place value
place-value chart

THINK

1. Write 15 on the place-value charts in two different ways.

15
Tens	Ones

15
Tens	Ones

2. Fill in the blank.

18 = 0 tens _____ ones

ENGAGE

Take more than 10 ▮▮▮▮.

How many ▮▮▮▮ are there?

Use your ▮▮▮▮ to make a bundle of 10.

How many ▮▮▮▮ are left?

Finish the sentence: _____ is the same as

_____ ten and _____ ones.

LEARN Use place value to show numbers to 20

1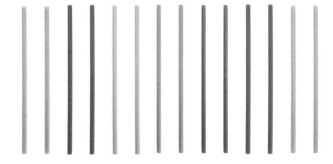

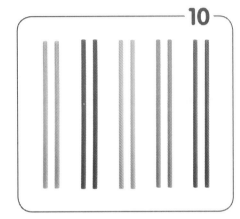 

10

I have one group of 10 and 4 left over.

This is a place-value chart.

Tens	Ones
1	4

14 = 1 ten 4 ones

2

13 = 1 ten 3 ones

Tens	Ones
1	3

Hands-on Activity Using place value to show numbers to 20

Work in pairs.

① Take some 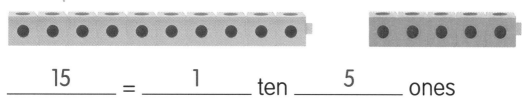.
Group your 🧊 into a ten and ones.

② **Mathematical Habit 7** Make use of structure

Ask your partner to write the number shown.

Example:

_____15_____ = _____1_____ ten _____5_____ ones

③ Trade places.
Repeat ① and ②.

_____ = _____ ten _____ ones

_____ = _____ ten _____ ones

_____ = _____ ten _____ ones

_____ = _____ ten _____ ones

_____ = _____ ten _____ ones

TRY Practice using place value to show numbers to 20

Write each missing number.

1

 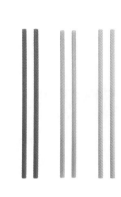

10

16 = _____ ten _____ ones

Tens	Ones

2

15 = _____ ten _____ ones

Tens	Ones

Circle the ▬▬▬ to show 1 ten 7 ones.

3

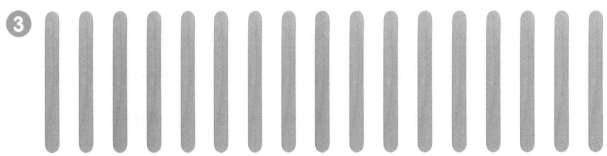

Circle the 🧊 to show 1 ten 2 ones.

4

INDEPENDENT PRACTICE

Write each missing number.

1

_____ ten _____ ones

Tens	Ones

Match.

2

•

•

Tens	Ones
1	2

•

•

Tens	Ones
1	9

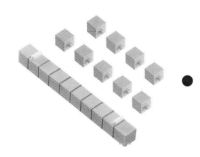

•

•

Tens	Ones
1	3

Write each missing number.

3 18 = _____ ten _____ ones

4 _____ = 1 ten 4 ones

Make a ✔ if the pair matches.
Make an ✘ if the pair does not match.

5

Tens	Ones
1	8

(   )

6

Tens	Ones
1	5

(   )

7

Tens	Ones
2	0

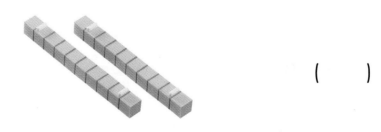

(   )

8

Tens	Ones
1	7

(   )

3 Comparing and Ordering Numbers

Learning Objectives:
- Compare numbers to 20.
- Order numbers to 20.

New Vocabulary
greater than (>)
less than (<)
greatest
least

THINK

A number is greater than 15 but less than 19.
a   Make a list of three numbers.
b   The digits in the number add to 8.
    What is the number?
Talk about how you find the answers with your partner.

ENGAGE

a   Use  to show this story:
    Lydia puts 18 in a row.
    Max puts 12 in a row.
    He matches each of his to each of Lydia's.
b   Who has more ?
c   How many must be changed to so that they are equal in number?

LEARN Use place value to compare and order numbers

1 Compare 13 and 15.

13

15

Tens	Ones	Tens	Ones
1	3	1	5

First, compare the tens.
They are equal.
Then, compare the ones.

5 ones are greater than 3 ones.
So, 15 is greater than 13.
You can write 15 > 13.

3 ones are less than 5 ones.
So, 13 is less than 15.
You can write 13 < 15.

">" means greater than.
"<" means less than.

2

Tens	Ones
1	2

Tens	Ones
1	2

The tens and the ones are the same.
12 is equal to 12.
You can write 12 = 12.

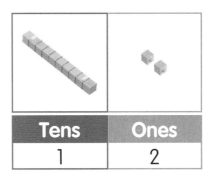

Math Talk
Is 1 ten 2 ones the same as 12 ones?

3 Compare 14, 11, and 16.

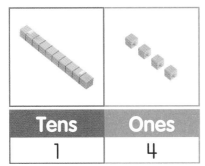

Tens	Ones
1	4

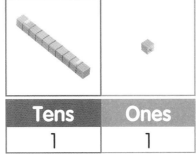

Tens	Ones
1	1

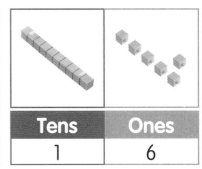

Tens	Ones
1	6

16 is the **greatest** number.
11 is the **least** number.
Order the numbers from least to greatest:

First, compare the tens.
They are the same.
Next, compare the ones.
6 ones are greater than 4 ones.
4 ones are greater than 1 one.

11 14 16
least   greatest

4 Order 15, 20, and 9 from greatest to least.

Tens	Ones
2	0
1	5
0	9

First, compare the tens.
2 tens is the greatest.
0 tens is the least.
So, 20 is the greatest.
9 is the least.

20   15   9

greatest   least

Hands-on Activity Ordering three numbers

Take some .

1 Use to make number trains to show 15, 8, and 13.

2 Order 15, 8, and 13 from greatest to least.
Use the number trains to help you.

_____, _____, _____

  greatest   least

3 Repeat 1 and 2 for 18, 19, and 16.

_____, _____, _____

  greatest   least

TRY Practice using place value to compare and order numbers

Fill in each blank.

1 Which is greater, 19 or 17?

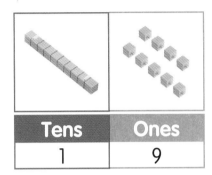

Tens	Ones
1	9

Tens	Ones
1	7

_____ is greater than _____.

2 Which is less, 16 or 12?

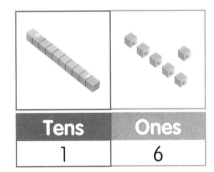

Tens	Ones
1	6

Tens	Ones
1	2

_____ is less than _____.

Fill in each blank with <, >, or =.

3 12 ◯ 15

4 13 ◯ 13

5 18 ◯ 12

6 16 ◯ 14

Compare the numbers.
Fill in each blank.

10   17   12

Tens	Ones		Tens	Ones		Tens	Ones
1	0		1	7		1	2

7 _____ is the greatest number.

8 _____ is the least number.

Compare the tens.
Then, compare the ones.

Order the numbers from greatest to least.

9   20   2   13

_____, _____, _____
greatest   least

Compare the tens.
Are they the same?

Order the numbers from least to greatest.

10   10   18   8

_____, _____, _____
least   greatest

INDEPENDENT PRACTICE

Fill in each blank.

1 Which number is greater?

 17   or   20

_____ is greater than _____.

_____ > _____

2 Which number is less?

 13   or   18

_____ is less than _____.

_____ < _____

Compare the numbers.
Fill in each blank.

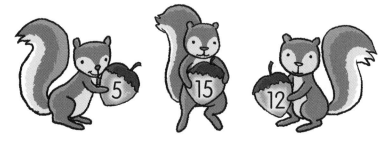

3 _____ is the greatest number.

4 _____ is the least number.

Order the numbers from greatest to least.

5

_____ , _____ , _____
greatest   least

Order the numbers from least to greatest.

6

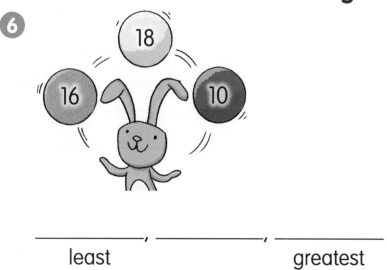

_____ , _____ , _____
least   greatest

The numbers are ordered from least to greatest.
What is the missing number?
Color all the likely answers.

7

Number Patterns

Learning Objectives:
- Find 1 more or 2 more than a number.
- Find 1 less or 2 less than a number.
- Find the missing numbers in a number pattern.

THINK

Write the missing numbers in each number pattern.

1 0, 2, 3, 5, 6, 8, 9, ___, ___

2 16, 15, 13, 12, 10, 9, 7, ___, ___

ENGAGE

1 a Use 12 🧱 to make a number train.
      After adding 1 🧱 to the train, it has ___ 🧱.

   b After adding 2 more 🧱 to the train, it has ___ 🧱.

2 Use 7 🧱 to make a number train.
   Add 🧱 to the train, two at a time.
   The number train has 17 🧱 in the end.
   How many times did you add the 🧱?

LEARN Find 1 more or 2 more than a number

1 What is 1 more than 13?

1 more

1 more than 13 is 14.

2 What is 2 more than 14?

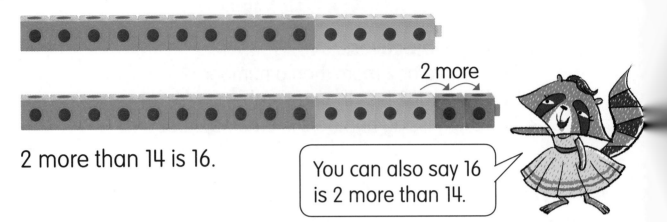

2 more

2 more than 14 is 16.

You can also say 16 is 2 more than 14.

TRY Practice finding 1 more or 2 more than a number

Fill in each blank.

1 What is 1 more than 15?

1 more

1 more than 15 is _____.

2 What is 2 more than 16?

2 more

2 more than 16 is _____.

ENGAGE

1 **a** Use 15 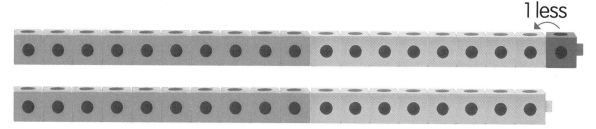 to make a number train.

  After taking away 1 🟦, the train has ___ 🟦.

  b After taking away 2 more 🟦, the train has ___ 🟦.

2 Use 18 🟦 to make a number train.

  Take away 🟦 from the train, two at a time.

  The number train has 6 🟦 left in the end.

  How many times did you take away the 🟦?

LEARN Find 1 less or 2 less than a number

1 What is 1 less than 19?

1 less

1 less than 19 is 18.

2 What is 2 less than 13?

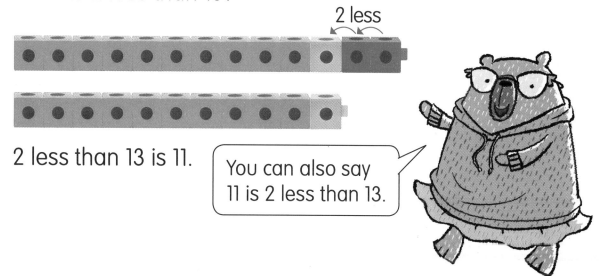

2 less

2 less than 13 is 11.

You can also say
11 is 2 less than 13.

TRY Practice finding 1 less or 2 less than a number

1 What is 1 less than 18?

1 less than 18 is _____.

2 What is 2 less than 14?

2 less than 14 is _____.

ENGAGE

Use 🎲 to make the pattern below.

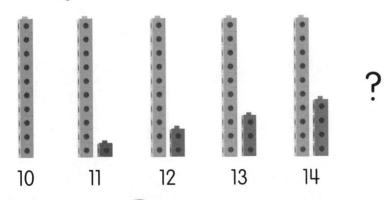

How many 🎲 come next in the pattern?
Talk about how you find the answer with your partner.

LEARN Find missing numbers in a number pattern

1 What comes next in the number pattern?
11, 12, 13, 14, 15, ?

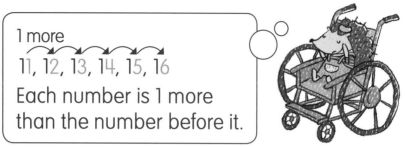

1 more
11, 12, 13, 14, 15, 16
Each number is 1 more
than the number before it.

16 comes next in the number pattern.

2 What comes next in the number pattern?
7, 9, 11, 13, 15, ?

2 more
7, 9, 11, 13, 15, 17
Each number is 2 more than
the number before it.

17 comes next in the number pattern.

3 What comes next in the number pattern?
17, 16, 15, 14, 13, ?

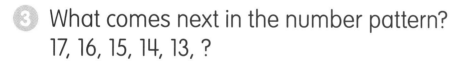

1 less
17, 16, 15, 14, 13, 12
Each number is 1 less
than the number before it.

12 comes next in the number pattern.

4 What comes next in the number pattern?
19, 17, 15, 13, 11, ?

> 2 less
>
> 19, 17, 15, 13, 11, 9
>
> Each number is 2 less
> than the number before it.

9 comes next in the number pattern.

Hands-on Activity Making number patterns

Work in groups of three.

1 Write a number to start.

2 Ask your classmate to write another number.
This number must be 1 more, 2 more, 1 less, or 2 less than
the first number.

3 **Mathematical Habit** 8 Look for patterns

Ask the other classmate to write a number to make a
number pattern.

4 **Mathematical Habit** 8 Look for patterns

Take turns to write a number to continue the
number pattern.

© 2020 Marshall Cavendish Education Pte Ltd

TRY Practice finding missing numbers in a number pattern

Look at the pattern.
Write the number of beads that comes next.

1

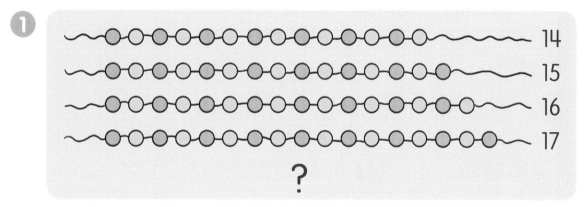

There are _____ beads in the next pattern.

Write the missing numbers in each number pattern.

2 10 11 12 13 ◯ ◯ ◯

Each number is 1 more than the one before it.

3 5 7 9 11 ◯ ◯ ◯

Each number is 2 more than the one before it.

4 20 19 18 17 ◯ ◯ ◯

5 18 16 14 12 ◯ ◯ ◯

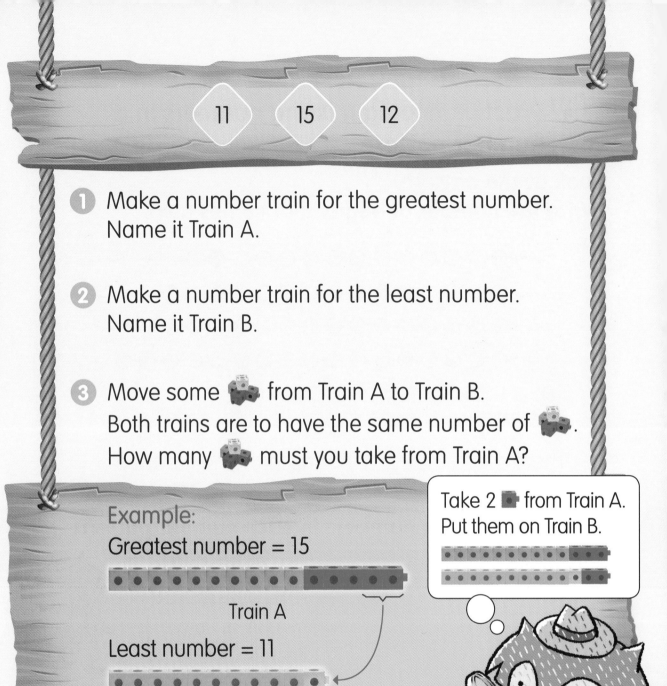

11   15   12

1. Make a number train for the greatest number.
   Name it Train A.

2. Make a number train for the least number.
   Name it Train B.

3. Move some 🔲 from Train A to Train B.
   Both trains are to have the same number of 🔲.
   How many 🔲 must you take from Train A?

Take 2 🔲 from Train A.
Put them on Train B.

Example:
Greatest number = 15

Train A

Least number = 11

Train B

4. Repeat 1 to 3 for these numbers.

a

16   11   19

b

20   12   17

Name: _____   Date: _____

INDEPENDENT PRACTICE

Write each missing number.

1. 1 more than 12 is _____.

2. 1 less than 16 is _____.

3. _____ is 2 more than 15.

4. _____ is 2 less than 14.

Write the missing numbers in each number pattern.

5.

6.

7.

8

Make a ✔ if the numbers make a pattern.
Make an ✗ if the numbers do not make a pattern.

9 8, 9, 10, 11, 12, 13   (   )

10 11, 12, 13, 15, 17, 18   (   )

11 15, 14, 13, 12, 11, 10   (   )

Make a number pattern with these numbers.

12

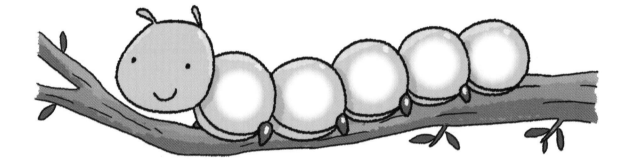

Name: _____ Date: _____

Mathematical Habit 2 Use mathematical reasoning

Show different ways to compare and order these numbers.

Problem Solving with Heuristics

1 **Mathematical Habit** **1** **Persevere in solving problems**

Use all six cards to make a number pattern.
What are the other two numbers that you need?

There is more than one correct answer!

2 **Mathematical Habit** **1** Persevere in solving problems

Each letter stands for a number.
Arrange the letters from least to greatest.

Use numbers in place of letters.

C is greater than A.
A is less than B.
C is less than B.

_____, _____, _____
    least   greatest

CHAPTER WRAP-UP

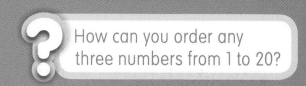

How can you order any three numbers from 1 to 20?

Numbers to 20

- Counting
- Reading and Writing
- Place Value
- Comparing and Ordering
- Number Patterns

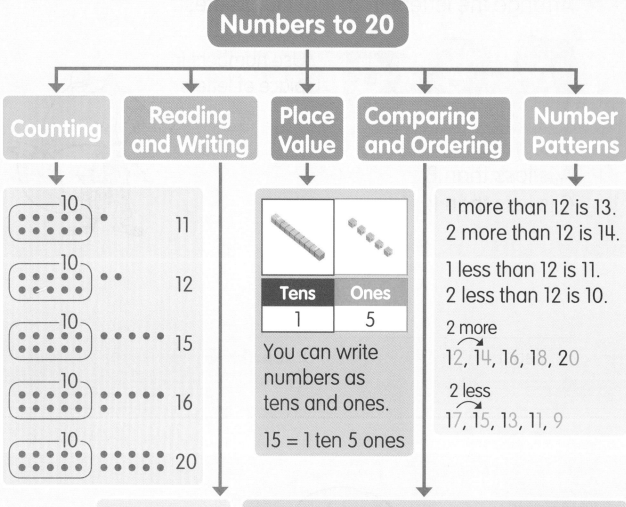

Counting

10 • 11
10 •• 12
10 •••• 15
10 ••••• 16
10 •••••• 20

Place Value

Tens	Ones
1	5

You can write numbers as tens and ones.

15 = 1 ten 5 ones

Number Patterns

1 more than 12 is 13.
2 more than 12 is 14.

1 less than 12 is 11.
2 less than 12 is 10.

2 more
12, 14, 16, 18, 20

2 less
17, 15, 13, 11, 9

Reading and Writing

11 eleven
12 twelve
13 thirteen
14 fourteen
15 fifteen
16 sixteen
17 seventeen
18 eighteen
19 nineteen
20 twenty

Comparing and Ordering

First, compare the tens.
The tens are equal.

Then, compare the ones.
8 ones are greater than 5 ones.
3 ones are less than 5 ones.

	Tens	Ones
13	1	3
18	1	8
15	1	5

So, 18 is the greatest.
13 is the least.

Order the numbers from greatest to least:
18, 15, 13

Name: _____ Date: _____

Make a 10.
Next, count on.
Then, write each number and word.

1

Number _____   Word _____

Fill in each blank.

2

10 and _____ make _____.

10 + _____ = _____

3 10 and _____ make 15.

Write each number.

4 seventeen _____

5 thirteen _____

Write each word.

6 11 _____

7 20 _____

Count.
Then, solve.

8 How many 🍍 are there?

Write the number.

Tens	Ones

9 Show the number.

Draw ▯ for tens and □ for ones.

**Compare the numbers.
Then, fill in each blank.**

10 Which number is greater?
Which number is less?

15   12

_____ > _____

_____ < _____

11 Which number is the greatest?
Which number is the least?

13   18   16

_____ is the greatest number.

_____ is the least number.

Order the numbers from least to greatest.

12   14   5   11

_____, _____, _____
least   greatest

Order the numbers from greatest to least.

13   16   10   20

_____, _____, _____
greatest   least

Fill in each blank.

14 2 less than 20 is _____.

15 _____ is 2 more than 9.

Find the missing numbers in each number pattern.

16

17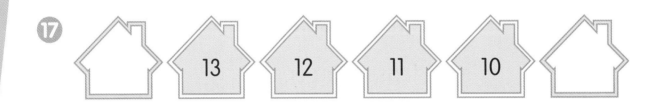

Assessment Prep
Answer each question.

18 Which numbers are ordered from least to greatest?
Color the boxes.

16, 17, 18, 19	17, 16, 15, 14
12, 13, 16, 14	11, 13, 16, 18

19 Which numbers are greater than 12 but less than 18?
Color the circles.

Fruits and Animals in a Garden

1 How many apples are there?

_____ and _____ make _____.

_____ + _____ = _____

There are _____ apples.

2 How many  are there?

a   Draw ▯ for tens and ☐ for ones.

b _____ = _____ ten _____ ones

3 The place-value charts show the number of deer and rabbits.
Are there fewer deer or rabbits?

Number of deer   Number of rabbits

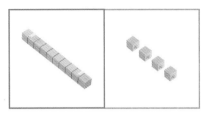 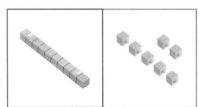

a _____ < _____

There are fewer _____. (deer / rabbits)

b How many fewer? _____ fewer

c How do you know?

_____

_____

4 Which tree has the greatest number of apples?
Read the clues to find out.

Clues
Tree A has 10 apples.
Tree B has 8 more apples than Tree A.
Tree C has 1 fewer apple than Tree B.

a Tree B has _____ apples.

b Tree C has _____ apples.

c Tree _____ has the greatest number of apples.

Rubric

Point(s)	Level	My Performance
7–8	4	• Most of my answers are correct. • I show all my work correctly. • I explain my thinking clearly and completely.
5–6.5	3	• Some of my answers are correct. • I show some of my work correctly. • I explain my thinking clearly.
3–4.5	2	• A few of my answers are correct. • I show little work correctly. • I explain some of my thinking clearly.
0–2.5	1	• A few of my answers are correct. • I show little or no work. • I do not explain my thinking clearly.

Teacher's Comments

Chapter 5
Addition and Subtraction Within 20

I can tell an addition story about the birds.

I can tell a subtraction story about the children.

How can you add and subtract two numbers?
What are the ways you can use?

Name: _____   Date: _____

Adding within 10

Add.
Use number bonds to help you.

a

$4 + 2 = 6$ or $2 + 4 = 6$
$4 + 2 = 2 + 4$
There are 6 whales in all.

Add.
Count on from the greater number.

b

Count on from the greater number to add.

2 steps

$5 + 2 = 7$
There are 7 jellyfish in all.

▶ **Quick Check**

Add.
Use number bonds to help you.

①

_____ + _____ = _____ or

_____ + _____ = _____

There are _____ polar bears in all.

Add.
Count on from the greater number.

②

5 + 3 = _____

There are _____ sea lions in all.

Subtracting within 10

There are 6 bears.
2 bears walk away.

2 steps

| 4 | 5 | 6 |

$6 - 2 = 4$

I can count back to subtract.

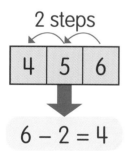

whole · 2 part
6
4 part

$6 - 2 = 4$
There are 4 bears left in the water.

I can use number bonds to help me subtract too!

▶ **Quick Check**

Subtract.
Count back from the greater number.

③ 9 − 2 = _____

6	7	8	9

Subtract.
Use number bonds to help you.

④ How many turtles are still in the sea?

_____ − _____ = _____

_____ turtles are still in the sea.

Making fact families

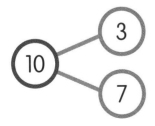

3 + 7 = 10
7 + 3 = 10
10 − 3 = 7
10 − 7 = 3

This is a
fact family.

▶ **Quick Check**

Make a fact family.

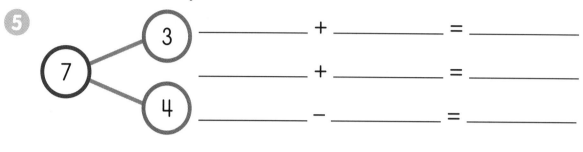

5 ⬤ 7 → 3, 4

_____ + _____ = _____

_____ + _____ = _____

_____ − _____ = _____

_____ − _____ = _____

Comparing numbers

Compare 13 and 11.

13

11

13 is greater than 11.
11 is less than 13.

▶ **Quick Check**

Write each missing number.

_____

_____

6 _____ is greater than _____.

7 _____ is less than _____.

Making addition and subtraction stories

You can make addition and subtraction stories about a picture.

There are 8 birds.
2 birds join them.

$8 + 2 = 10$
There are 10 birds in all.

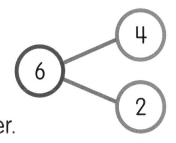

There are 6 dolphins.
2 dolphins jump out
of the water.

$6 - 2 = 4$
4 dolphins are in the water.

▶ **Quick Check**

**Make an addition story.
Then, write each missing number.**

⑧

_____ otters are in the water.

_____ otters are out of the water.

_____ + _____ = _____

There are _____ otters in all.

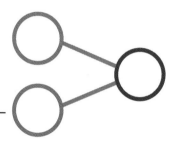

**Make a subtraction story.
Then, write each missing number.**

⑨

There are _____ penguins in all.

_____ penguins are swimming.

_____ – _____ = _____

_____ penguins are on land.

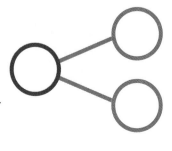

Ways to Add Fluently

Learning Objectives:
- Add by counting on.
- Add by making a 10.
- Add by using doubles and doubles plus one facts.
- Understand that addition can be done in any order.

New Vocabulary
group
doubles facts
doubles plus one facts

THINK

$7 +$ _____ $= 15$
Find the missing number.
Use two different ways to find the answer.

ENGAGE

a   Juan's backyard has 11 plants.
He adds another 3 plants to his backyard, one at a time.
How many plants does he have now?

b   If Juan has 15 plants in his backyard in the end, how many plants were added?

Talk about how you find your answers with your partner.

LEARN Add by counting on

1. Landon has 12 toy dinosaurs.
Hailey gives him another 3 toy dinosaurs.
How many toy dinosaurs does Landon have in all?

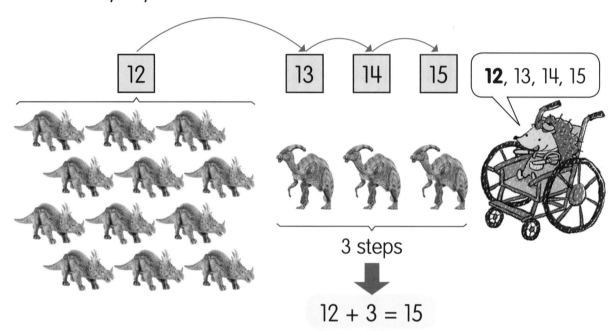

12, 13, 14, 15

3 steps

12 + 3 = 15

Landon has 15 toy dinosaurs in all.

Math Talk

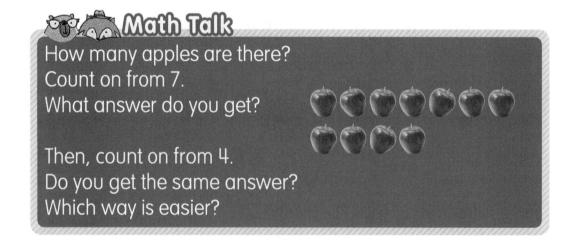

How many apples are there?
Count on from 7.
What answer do you get?

Then, count on from 4.
Do you get the same answer?
Which way is easier?

TRY Practice counting on to add

Add.
Count on from the greater number.

1

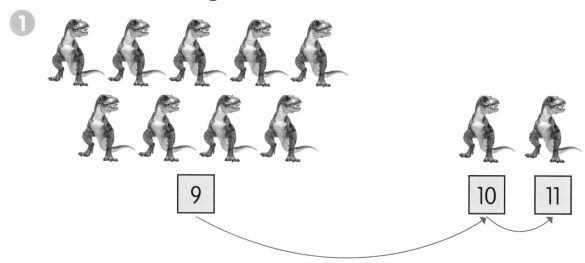

9

10   11

$9 + 2 = $ _____

Add.
Count on from the greater number.
Draw arrows to help you.

2   $13 + 4 = $ _____

13	14	15	16	17	18	19	20

3   $9 + 3 = $ _____

9	10	11	12	13	14

ENGAGE

Use 7 🔲 and 5 🔲 to make two number trains
Show two ways to make a 10 with your number trains.
Write a number bond to show each way.
How many 🔲 are there in all?

LEARN Add by making a 10

1 Violeta has 8 cherries.
Thomas gives her 6 cherries.
How many cherries does Violeta have now?

STEP 1 Make a group of 10 cherries.

8   +   6

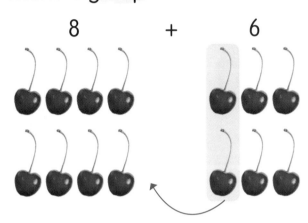

> Break the number that is less into two parts.
> 8 + 6 = 14
>
> 2   4
> 8 and 2 make 10.
> 10 and 4 make 14.

STEP 2 Add the rest of the cherries to the group of 10.

10   +   4

10 + 4 = 14
Violeta has 14 cherries now.

Hands-on Activity Making a 10 to add

Take some  .

① Use  to show these numbers. | 9 | 3 |

② Add 9 and 3.
Group the  to make a 10.
Then, add.
Example:

9 + 3

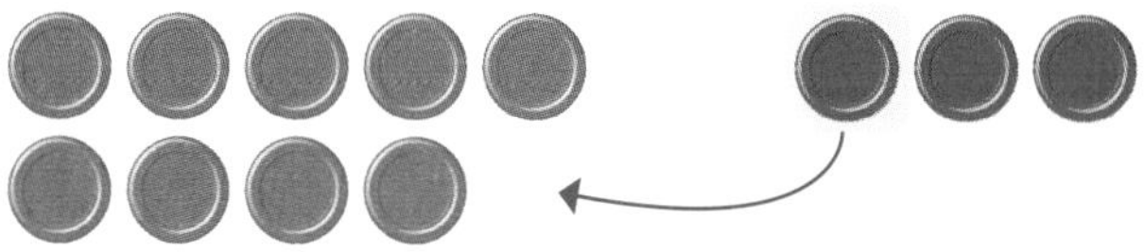

9 and 1 make 10.
10 and 2 make 12.

10 + 2

9 + 3 = 12

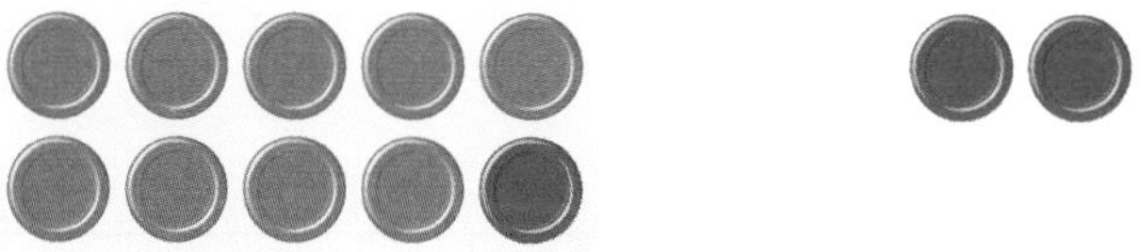

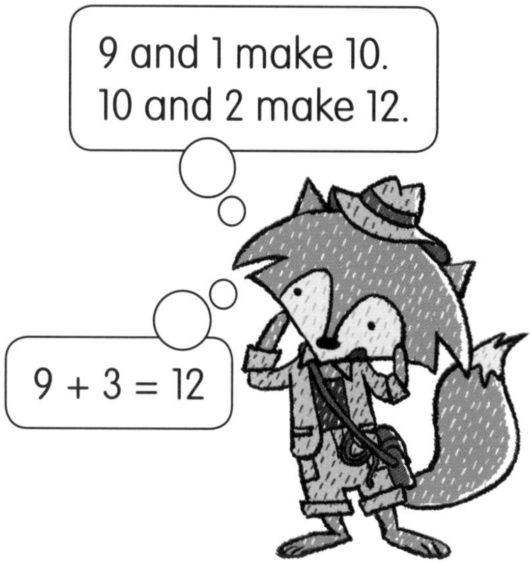

9 + 3 = _____

③ Repeat ① and ② for these number sentences.

a   8 + 6 = _____

8 + 6

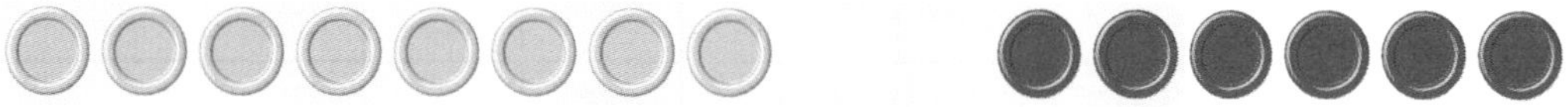

b   7 + 6 = _____   7 + 6

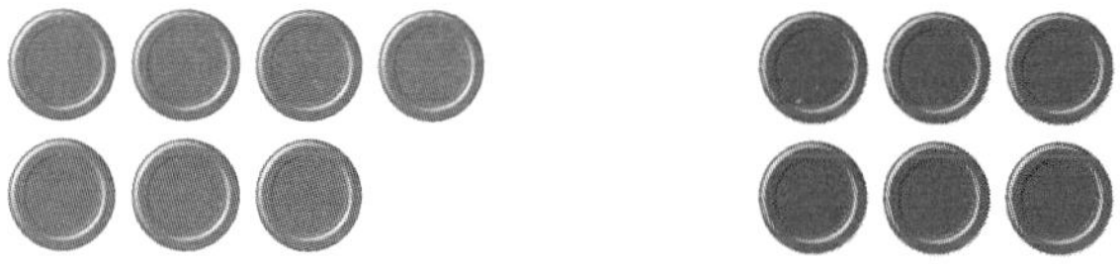

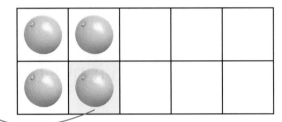 TRY Practice making a 10 to add

Make a 10.
Then, add.

1

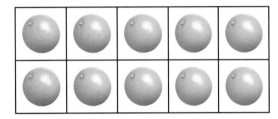 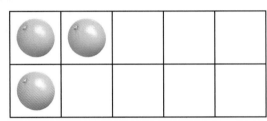

⬇

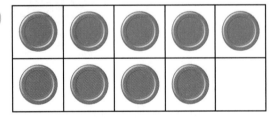 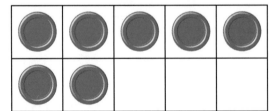

9 + 4 = _____

2

⬇

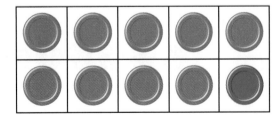 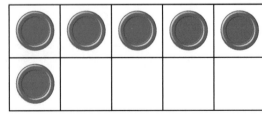

9 + 7 = _____

3 $9 + 5 = $ _____

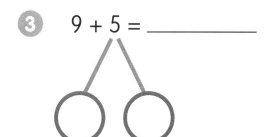

4 $7 + 7 = $ _____

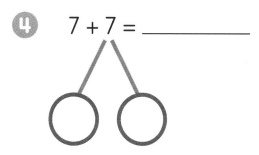

Mathematical Habit 3 Construct viable arguments

Marco has 8 T-shirts.
He buys another 7 T-shirts.
Marco uses the strategy below to find how many T-shirts he has now.

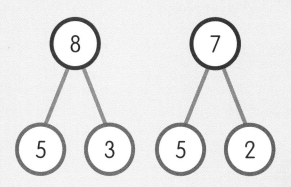

STEP **1** $\quad 5 + 5 = 10$

STEP **2** $\quad 3 + 2 = 5$

STEP **3** $\quad 10 + 5 = 15$

Talk about how Marco's strategy works with your partner.
Then, use his strategy to add 8 and 5.

MATH SHARING

ENGAGE

1 Use your fingers to show two numbers that make 10.
Then, complete the addition sentence.
$5 +$ _____ $= 10$

2 Use 🪙 to show each story:

a Ricardo has 5 ● and 4 ●.
How can he use 🪙 to make a 10?

b Sofia has 5 ● and 6 ●.
How can she use 🪙 to make a 10?

LEARN Add by using doubles and doubles plus one facts

1 This is a **doubles fact**.

$2 + 2 = 4$

Double 2 means to add 2 more to 2.
The numbers to be added are the same.

2 Here are some other doubles facts.

$3 + 3 = 6$

$4 + 4 = 8$

$5 + 5 = 10$

Math Talk
How can you add two numbers that are the same?

3 What is 2 + 3?

2 + 3 = ?

2   1

You can rewrite 2 + 3 as 2 + 2 + 1.
So, 2 + 3 is a double 2 plus 1.
2 + 3 is a **doubles plus one fact**.

You can use the doubles fact of 2 + 2 to add 2 and 3.

doubles
2 + 2 = 4

doubles plus one
2 + 3 = 2 + 2 + 1
    = 4 + 1
    = 5

2 + 2 and 1 more

What other doubles plus one facts are there?

Hands-on Activity — Using doubles and doubles plus one facts to add

Work in pairs.

Your teacher will give you some cards and some 🔘.

① Take a card.

② Look at the addition sentence on your card.
Arrange two rows of 🔘 to show the sentence.

③ Ask your partner to find the answer using doubles or doubles plus one facts.

④ Trade places.
Repeat ① to ③ a few times.

TRY Practice using doubles or doubles plus one facts to add

Fill in each blank.

① Double 5 means add _____ more to 5.

② 5 + 5 = _____

Circle the doubles facts.
Cross the doubles plus one facts.

3 $4 + 4 = 8$ $4 + 5 = 9$ $8 + 7 = 15$ $7 + 7 = 14$

Write each missing number.

4 $5 + 6 = ?$

$5 + 6 = 5 +$ _____ $+$ _____

$\qquad = 10 +$ _____

$\qquad =$ _____

ENGAGE

1 Clara adds 7 and 5 in two different ways.

$7 + 5 =$ _____ $5 + 7 =$ _____

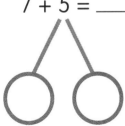   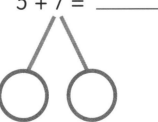

Talk about what you notice with your partner.

2 Find the value of $9 + 4$.
Without calculating, find the value of $4 + 9$.

LEARN Add in any order

1 How many  are there in all?

7 + 8 = ?

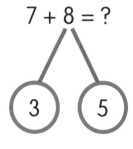

3   5

7 + 3 = 10
10 + 5 = 15

Make a 10 to add.

So, 7 + 8 = 15.

7 + 8 = 15
Is 8 + 7 = 15 too?
Let us find out!

8 + 7 = ?

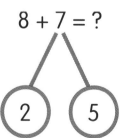

2   5

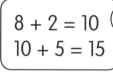

8 + 2 = 10
10 + 5 = 15

So, 8 + 7 = 15.

7 + 8 = 8 + 7
You can add in any order.

Hands-on Activity · Adding in any order

① Use 🎲 to make number trains for 9 and 6.
Use only one color for each train.

② **Mathematical Habit 7** Make use of structure

Rearrange the 🎲 to show two ways to make a 10.
Then, add 9 and 6.

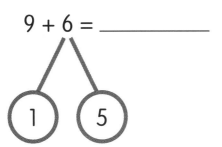

9 + 6 = _____

1   5

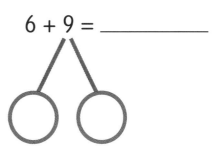

6 + 9 = _____

③ Repeat ① and ② for these addition sentences.

a   9 + 5 = _____

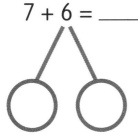

5 + 9 = _____

b   7 + 6 = _____

6 + 7 = _____

TRY Practice adding in any order

Fill in each blank.

1

$5 + 8 =$ _____

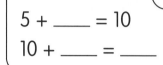
5 + ____ = 10
10 + ____ = ____

$8 + 5 =$ _____

8 + ____ = 10
10 + ____ = ____

Is $8 + 5 = 5 + 8$? _____

Write each missing number.

You can add in any order!

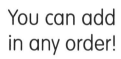

2 $10 + 4 =$ _____ $+ 10$

3 $6 +$ _____ $= 9 + 6$

4 _____ $+ 5 = 5 + 7$

INDEPENDENT PRACTICE

Add.
Count on from the greater number.
Draw arrows to help you.

1

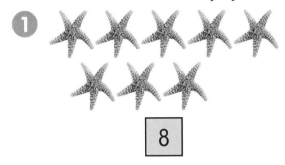 8

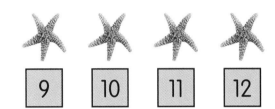 9 10 11 12

8 + 4 = _____

2

13

 14 15 16

13 + 3 = _____

Add.
Count on from the greater number.
Use the counting tape to help you.

7	8	9	10	11	12	13	14	15	16	17	18	19	20

3 13 + 2 = _____

4 16 + 3 = _____

5 9 + 3 = _____

6 7 + 4 = _____

Make a 10.
Then, add.

7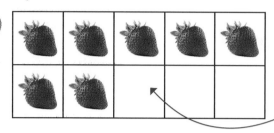

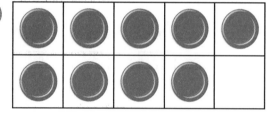 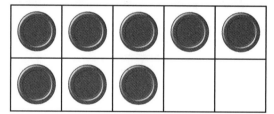

$7 + 5 = $ _____

8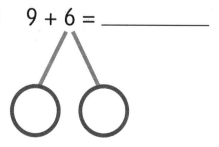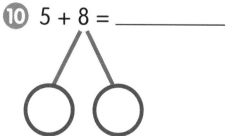

$9 + 8 = $ _____

Make a 10.
Then, add.

9 $9 + 6 = $ _____

10 $5 + 8 = $ _____

Fill in each blank.

⑪ Double 6 is _____ + _____ = _____.

⑫ 6 + 7 = _____ + _____ + _____

  = _____

⑬ What doubles fact helps you to add 9 and 8? _____

⑭ 8 + 9 = _____

Add.
Then, write the missing number in each ☐.

⑮

+	3	4	5	6	7	8	9
3		7	8	9	10	11	12
4			9	10	11	12	13
5				11	12	13	14
6					13	14	15
7						15	16
8							17
9							

You can add in any order!

Draw lines to match the same answers.

16

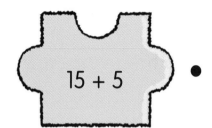

12 + 4

9 + 10

15 + 5

8 + 8

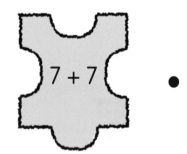

7 + 7

5 + 8

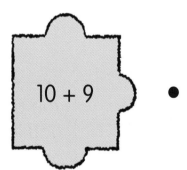

10 + 9

5 + 9

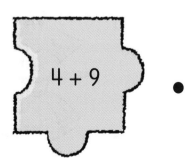

4 + 9

10 + 10

2 Ways to Subtract Fluently

Learning Objectives:
- Subtract by counting back.
- Subtract by grouping into a 10 and ones.
- Recognize related addition and subtraction sentences.
- Make fact families from number sentences.
- Subtract by using addition facts.
- Determine if number sentences involving addition and subtraction are true or false.

 THINK

Find each missing number.

a $15 -$ _____ $= 9$

b   _____ $- 8 = 9$

Talk about how you find each missing number with your partner.

ENGAGE

Malik has 16 markers.

a   He gives a marker to each of the 3 students at his table, one at a time.
    How many markers does he have left?

b   If Malik has 10 markers left, how many markers does each student receive?

Talk about how you find your answers with your partner.

LEARN Subtract by counting back

1 Anthony has 17 toy cars.
He gives away 3 toy cars.
How many toy cars does Anthony have left?

$17 - 3 = ?$

Start from 17.
Count back 3 steps.

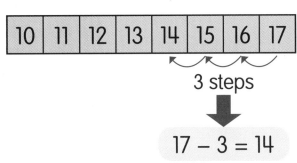

| 10 | 11 | 12 | 13 | 14 | 15 | 16 | 17 |

3 steps

$17 - 3 = 14$

17, 16, 15, 14

Anthony has 14 toy cars left.

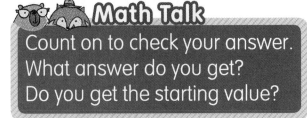

Math Talk

Count on to check your answer.
What answer do you get?
Do you get the starting value?

① Use the counting tape to help you count back 3 steps.

| 14 | 15 | 16 | 17 | 18 |

18 − 3 = _____

② Check your answer.
Count on 3 steps from your answer.

Check: _____ + 3 = _____

③ Make a counting tape ending with 15.

④ Write a subtraction sentence.
Use the counting tape you made to help you.

Check: _____ − _____ = _____

⑤ Count on to check your answer.

_____ + _____ = _____

⑥ Repeat ③ to ⑤ for 20.

_____ − _____ = _____

Check: _____ + _____ = _____

TRY Practice counting back to subtract

Subtract.
Count back from the greater number.
Draw arrows to help you.

1

$14 - 2 =$ _____

11	12	13	14

2 $18 - 4 =$ _____

11	12	13	14	15	16	17	18

Subtract.
Count back from the greater number.
Then, color the ⬭ **with the same answers in the same color.**

3

$20 - 3 =$ _____

$16 - 3 =$ _____

$20 - 2 =$ _____

$19 - 3 =$ _____

$20 - 4 =$ _____

$19 - 2 =$ _____

$17 - 4 =$ _____

$18 - 2 =$ _____

$18 - 0 =$ _____

ENGAGE

1 Use 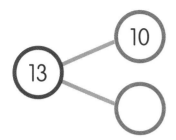 to help you complete each number bond.

 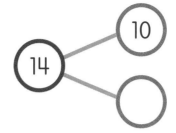 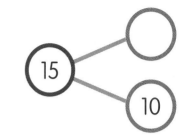

2 Find each missing number.
Use number bonds to help you.

a   12 – _____ = 7   b   _____ – 4 = 12

LEARN Subtract by grouping into a 10 and ones

1 Samuel makes 12 stars.
He gives 7 stars to Amirah.
How many stars does Samuel have left?

STEP 1   12 is 10 and 2.

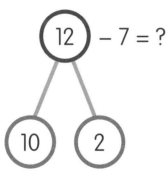

$$12 - 7 = ?$$

STEP 2   You cannot subtract 7 from 2.
So, subtract 7 from 10.
10 – 7 = 3

STEP 3   Add 2 and 3.
2 + 3 = 5
So, 12 – 7 = 5.
Samuel has 5 stars left.

TRY Practice grouping into a 10 and ones to subtract

Subtract.

1 10 – 4 = _____

2 10 – 7 = _____

Group each number into a 10 and ones.
Then, subtract.

3

12 – 4 = _____

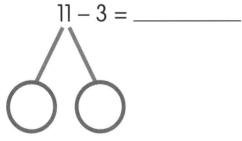

4 11 – 3 = _____

5 13 – 6 = _____

6 14 – 8 = _____

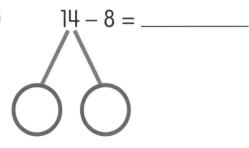

7 15 – 7 = _____

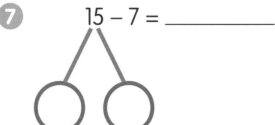

Mathematical Habit 3 Construct viable arguments

Ana uses this way to subtract 5 from 12.

STEP 1

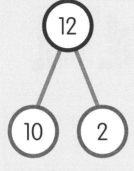 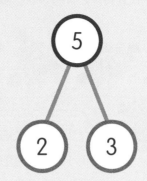

STEP 2 12 − 2 = 10

STEP 3 10 − 3 = 7

So, 12 − 5 = 7.
Talk about how Ana's way works with your partner.
Then, use her way to subtract 8 from 12.

ENGAGE

1 Complete the number bond.
Then, make a fact family.

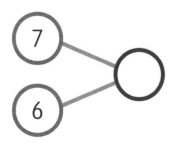

_____ + _____ = _____

_____ + _____ = _____

_____ − _____ = _____

_____ − _____ = _____

2 Use two ways to find each missing number.

a   15 − _____ = 7   b   _____ + 8 = 15

Talk about how you do it with your partner.

LEARN Subtract using addition facts

1 You can make a fact family from an addition sentence.

There are 7 pink roses.
There are 4 yellow roses.

$7 + 4 = 11$

7 + 4 = 11 is an addition fact. You can use this fact to write other related facts.

$7 + 4 = 11$ $11 - 7 = 4$
$4 + 7 = 11$ $11 - 4 = 7$

2 You can also make a fact family from a subtraction sentence.

$13 - 8 = 5$

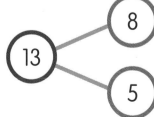

There are 13 .
8 are 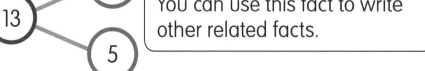.

13 − 8 = 5 is a subtraction fact. You can use this fact to write other related facts.

$13 - 8 = 5$ $8 + 5 = 13$
$13 - 5 = 8$ $5 + 8 = 13$

3 There are 12 deer.
8 deer are drinking from the pond.
How many deer are not drinking
from the pond?

$12 - 8 = ?$

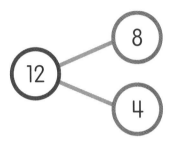

8 + 4 = 12 is the
related addition fact.

8 + 4 = 12
So, 12 − 8 = 4.

So, $12 - 8 = 4$.
4 deer are not drinking from the pond.

4 Emma has some balloons.
She gives Isaac 4 balloons.
She has 9 balloons left.
How many balloons does Emma have at first?

___?___ $- 4 = 9$

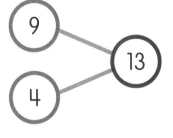
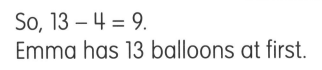

4 + 9 = 13 is the
related addition fact.

4 + 9 = 13.
So, 13 − 4 = 9.

So, $13 - 4 = 9$.
Emma has 13 balloons at first.

Hands-on Activity

Activity 1 Making fact families

Take two 🎲 **and some** 🔵.

① Roll each 🎲.

② **Mathematical Habit 7** Make use of structure

Write both numbers on the number bond.
Add the two numbers.
Use 🔵 to help you.
Then, complete the number bond and make a fact family.

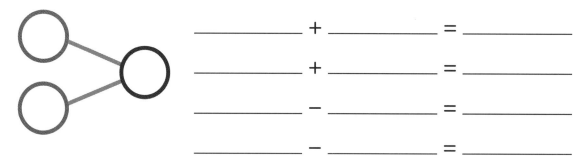

_____ + _____ = _____

_____ + _____ = _____

_____ − _____ = _____

_____ − _____ = _____

③ Choose a number from 6 to 10.
Choose another number from 11 to 20.

④ **Mathematical Habit 7** Make use of structure

Write both numbers on the number bond.
Subtract the two numbers.
Use 🔵 to help you.

Then, complete the number bond and make a fact family.

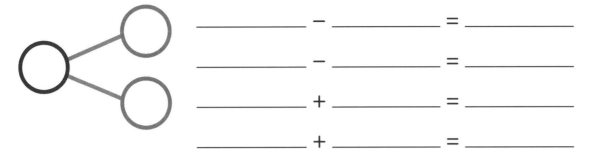

_____ − _____ = _____

_____ − _____ = _____

_____ + _____ = _____

_____ + _____ = _____

Activity 2 Using addition facts to subtract

Work in pairs.

Your teacher will provide you with two sets of cards and some 🪙 .

① Choose one card from each set.

② Count on or back to subtract the two numbers.
Use 🪙 to help you.

③ **Mathematical Habit 7** **Make use of structure**
Ask your partner to use an addition fact to help him or her subtract.

④ Compare your answers.
Do you and your partner have the same answer?

⑤ Trade places.
Repeat ① to ④ a few times.

TRY Practice using addition facts to subtract

Complete each number bond.
Then, make a fact family for each number sentence.

1

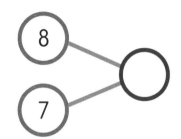

8 + 7 = _____ is
an addition fact.

8 + 7 = _____   _____ – _____ = _____

_____ + _____ = _____   _____ – _____ = _____

2

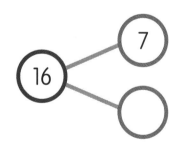

16 – 7 = _____ is
a subtraction fact.

16 – 7 = _____   _____ + _____ = _____

_____ – _____ = _____   _____ + _____ = _____

Fill in each blank.

3 Miguel has 12 eggs.
7 eggs are white.
How many eggs are brown?

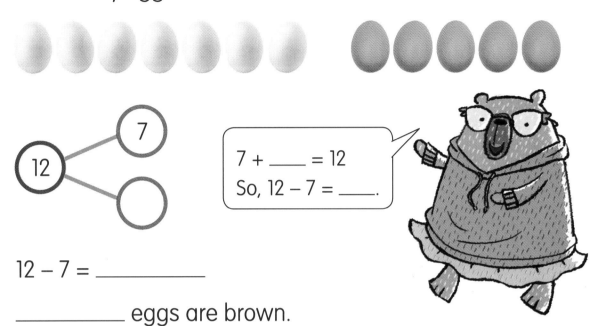

$7 + \underline{\quad} = 12$

So, $12 - 7 = \underline{\quad}$.

$12 - 7 = \underline{\hspace{3cm}}$

$\underline{\hspace{3cm}}$ eggs are brown.

4 There were some birds on a tree.
6 birds flew away.
8 birds are left on the tree.
How many birds were there in all?

$\underline{\hspace{2cm}}^{?} - 6 = 8$

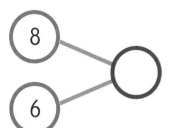

$8 + 6 = \underline{\quad}$

So, $\underline{\quad} - 6 = 8$.

$\underline{\hspace{3cm}} - 6 = 8$

There were $\underline{\hspace{2cm}}$ birds in all.

ENGAGE

Look at the number sentence.

16 − _____ = _____ + 6

What are some numbers that make the sentence true?
Use 🔵⚪ to help you find the numbers.

LEARN Tell if a number sentence is true or false

① Is 16 − 3 = 7 + 6 a true number sentence?

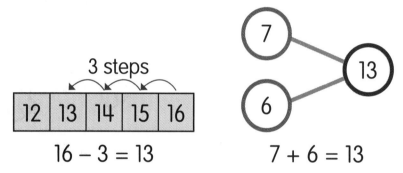

3 steps

| 12 | 13 | 14 | 15 | 16 |

16 − 3 = 13

7 + 6 = 13

Both number sentences have the same answer.
So, 16 − 3 = 7 + 6 is true.

② Is 11 − 3 = 12 − 5 a true number sentence?

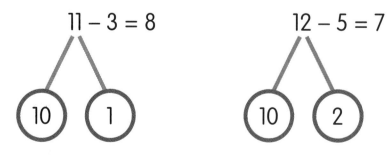

11 − 3 = 8

12 − 5 = 7

10 1

10 2

Both number sentences do not have the same answer.
So, 11 − 3 = 12 − 5 is false.

TRY Practice telling if a number sentence is true or false

Fill in each blank.

① Is 15 − 6 = 6 + 5 a true number sentence?

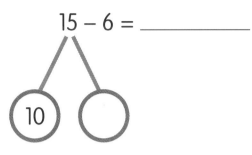

15 − 6 = _____

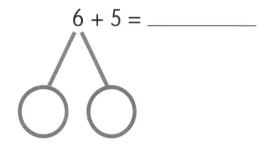

6 + 5 = _____

Do 15 − 6 and 6 + 5 have the same answer? _____

So, this number sentence is _____ (true / false).

② Is 14 + 2 = 19 − 3 a true number sentence?

14 + 2 = _____

14	15	16	17

19 − 3 = _____

15	16	17	18	19

Do 14 + 2 and 19 − 3 have the same answer? _____

So, this number sentence is _____ (true / false).

MATCH UP!

It is a match!

6+6

15-3

What you need:

Players: 2
Materials: Addition cards, Subtraction cards

What to do:

Arrange the cards face down on the table.

1. Player 1 turns over an addition card and
a subtraction card.
Keep the cards if they match.
Turn them back if they do not.

2. Trade places.
Repeat 1.

Who is the winner?

The first player to collect ten cards wins.

INDEPENDENT PRACTICE

Subtract.
Count back from the greater number.
Draw arrows to help you.

18 – 2 = _____

15	16	17	18

14 – 3 = _____

9	10	11	12	13	14

20 – 4 = _____

13	14	15	16	17	18	19	20

Subtract.
Count back from the greater number.
Then, draw lines to match each eagle to its nest.

20 − 2

1 3

19 − 3

1 0

16 − 3

1 8

14 − 4

1 6

Group each number into a 10 and ones.
Then, subtract.

14 − 5 = _____

10

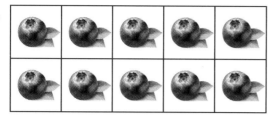

$$15 - 6 = \underline{\hspace{3cm}}$$

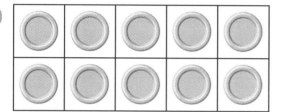

$$17 - 9 = \underline{\hspace{3cm}}$$

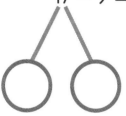

8 $\quad 11 - 4 = \underline{\hspace{3cm}}$

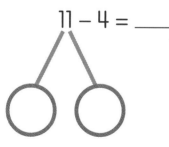

9 $\quad 18 - 9 = \underline{\hspace{3cm}}$

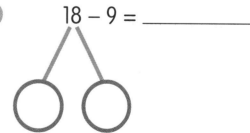

Look at each number sentence.
Complete the number bond.
Then, make a fact family.

10

9 + 6 = _____   _____ − _____ = _____

_____ + _____ = _____   _____ − _____ = _____

11

13 − 9 = _____   _____ + _____ = _____

_____ − _____ = _____   _____ + _____ = _____

Subtract.
Use a related addition fact to help you.
Write the related addition fact.

⑫ 14 – 6 = _____

Addition fact: _____ + 6 = 14

⑬ _____ – 7 = 4

Addition fact: _____ + _____ = _____

Subtract.
Color the piece with a different answer.

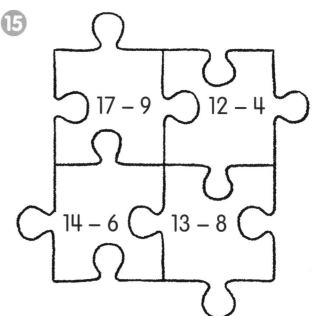

⑭

| 16 – 7 | 16 – 8 |
| 13 – 4 | 15 – 6 |

⑮

| 17 – 9 | 12 – 4 |
| 14 – 6 | 13 – 8 |

Look at each number sentence.
Is each number sentence true or false?
Add or subtract to find out.

16 17 − 8 = 12 − 3

17 − 8 = _____

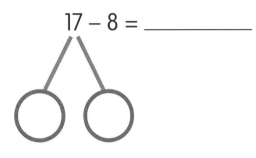

12 − 3 = _____

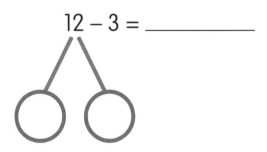

Do 17 − 8 and 12 − 3 have the same answer? _____

So, this number sentence is _____ (true / false).

17 5 + 7 = 12 − 2

5 + 7 = _____

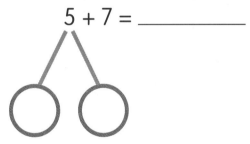

12 − 2 = _____

| 9 | 10 | 11 | 12 |

Do 5 + 7 and 12 − 2 have the same answer? _____

So, this number sentence is _____ (true / false).

Look at the number sentence.
Circle true or false.
If the sentence is false, change a number to make it true.

18 8 + 6 = 16 − 8   true / false

Correct number sentence _____

Name: _____   Date: _____

3 Real-World Problems: Addition and Subtraction

Learning Objective:
• Solve real-world problems involving addition and subtraction.

THINK

Sarah needs 18 long and short nails to make a shelf.
She needs more than 5 nails of each type.
She also needs more long nails than short nails.
How many long nails does Sarah need?
How many short nails does she need?
Give three answers.

ENGAGE

1. Decide if you need to add or subtract in each story.
   Talk about how you find your answers with your partner.

   a

   Jason takes away 7 cucumbers.
   How many cucumbers are there left?

   Use to help you.

   b

   Olivia buys 4 more tomatoes.
   How many tomatoes are there now?

2. Make a subtraction story using the word **more**.
   Make an addition story using the words **take away**.

LEARN Solve real-world problems involving addition and subtraction

1 Jade has 9 .
Rodrigo gives her 6 .
How many does Jade have in all?

STEP 1 Understand the problem.

How many does Jade have?
How many does Rodrigo give her?
What do I need to find?

STEP 2 Think of a plan.
I can act it out.

STEP 3 Carry out the plan.

$9 + 6 = 15$
Jade has 15 in all.

STEP 4 Check the answer.
I can solve it in another way.

$9 + 6 = 15$

1   5

2 Connor has 16 key chains.
He gives Ellie 5 key chains.
How many key chains does Connor have left?

16 – 5 = 11
Connor has 11 key chains left.

TRY Practice solving real-world problems involving addition and subtraction

Solve.

1 Carrie makes 6 kites.
Justin makes 6 kites.
How many kites do the children make in all?

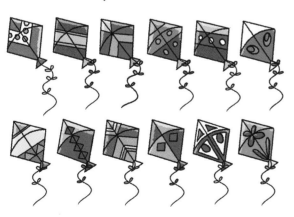

Use the four-step problem-solving model to help you.

_____ + _____ = _____

The children make _____ kites in all.

2 Angel has 11 paper clips.
3 paper clips are blue.
The rest are red.
How many paper clips are red?

_____ − _____ = _____

_____ paper clips are red.

3 Orion has 14 caps.
He gives away 7 caps.
How many caps does Orion have left?

_____ − _____ = _____

Orion has _____ caps left.

Mathematical Habit 4 Use mathematical models

Look at the picture.
Make an addition or a subtraction story.
Get your classmates to solve your story.

Example:

There are 12 students.
4 students have blonde hair.
How many students do not have blonde hair?

$12 - 4 = 8$
8 students do not have blonde hair.

Work in pairs.

| 15 | 13 | 14 | 12 | 16 |

1 Think of any two numbers to make
each number above.
How many ways can you do it?
Use 🎲 to help you.

| 5 | 6 | 7 | 8 | 9 | 13 | 15 |

2 Use the numbers above to make
fact families.
You can use each number more than once.
How many fact families can you make?

INDEPENDENT PRACTICE

Solve.

1 Jonathan has 13 stickers.
Abigail gives him another 6 stickers.
How many stickers does Jonathan have now?

_____ ◯ _____ = _____

Jonathan has _____ stickers now.

2 A store has 15 beanies.
3 beanies are sold.
How many beanies are left?

_____ ◯ _____ = _____

_____ beanies are left.

3 Cameron has 17 cookies.
He eats some and has 9 cookies left.
How many cookies does Cameron eat?

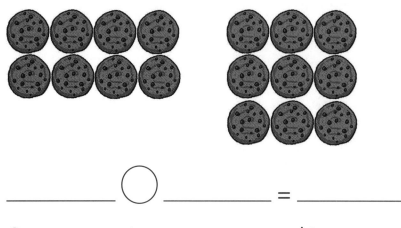

_____ ◯ _____ = _____

Cameron eats _____ cookies.

4 Ms. Howard has some watermelons in her store.
She sells 7 watermelons and has 6 watermelons left.
How many watermelons are there in the store at first?

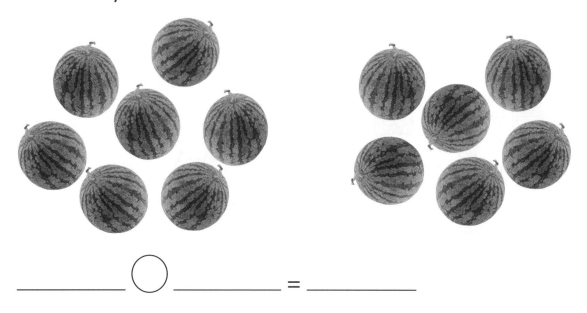

_____ ◯ _____ = _____

There are _____ watermelons in the store at first.

Name: _____ Date: _____

Mathematical Habit 3 Construct viable arguments

Look at the number sentence.

15 − 7 = 7 + 7

Is this number sentence true or false?

Write the steps to find out.

Problem Solving with Heuristics

1 **Mathematical Habit** **1** Persevere in solving problems

Fill in each blank with the numbers given.
You can only use each number once.

a Make three addition sentences using these numbers.

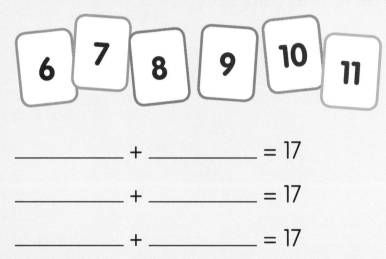

_____ + _____ = 17

_____ + _____ = 17

_____ + _____ = 17

b Make three subtraction sentences using these numbers.

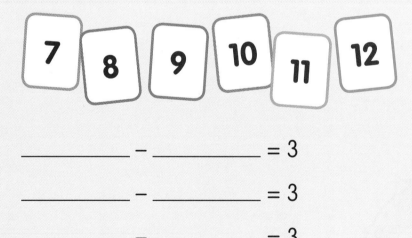

_____ − _____ = 3

_____ − _____ = 3

_____ − _____ = 3

2 **Mathematical Habit** **1** Persevere in solving problems

Catalina has two numbers.
When she adds them, she gets 13.
When she subtracts them, she gets 3.
What are the two numbers?

List the numbers.

3 Mathematical Habit 1 Persevere in solving problems

The mouse wants to find its way to the cheese.
The total value of the paths it takes must add to 20.
Each path can only be used once.
Draw arrows to show the mouse the correct way.

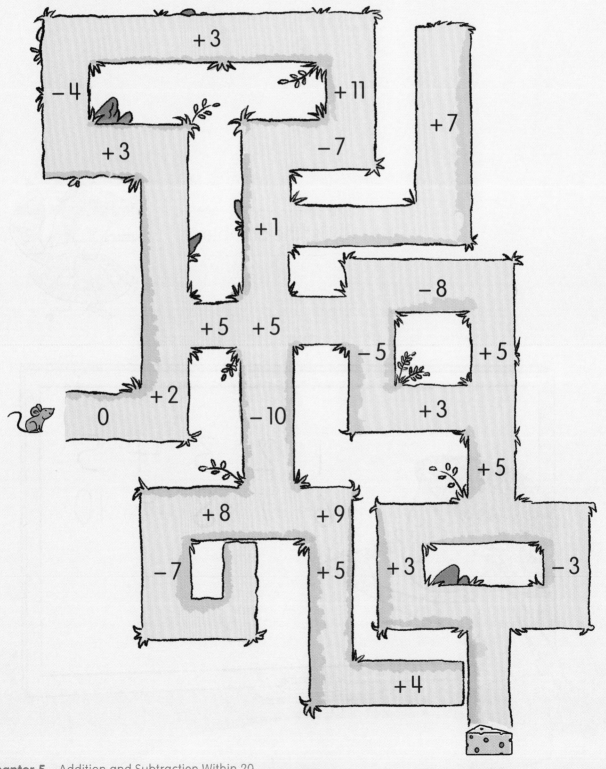

CHAPTER WRAP-UP

Addition Within 20

Ways to Add

You can count on from the greater number to add.

$9 + 4 = 13$

9	10	11	12	13	14

You can make a 10 to add.

$9 + 4$

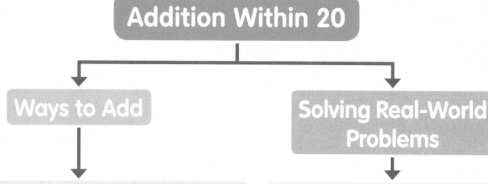

$9 + 1 = 10$
$10 + 3 = 13$

You can use doubles facts to add.
$3 + 3 = 6$ is a doubles fact.

You can use doubles plus one facts to add.
$3 + 4$ is $3 + 3 + 1$.
$3 + 4 = 3 + 3 + 1$
$\quad\quad = 7$

You can add in any order.
$9 + 3 = 12$ $\quad\quad$ $3 + 9 = 12$
So, $9 + 3 = 3 + 9$.

Solving Real-World Problems

Valery bakes 8 bread buns. Carlos bakes 4 bread buns. How many bread buns do both of them bake in all?

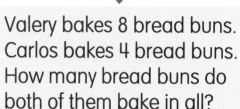

$8 + 4 = 12$
Both of them bake 12 bread buns in all.

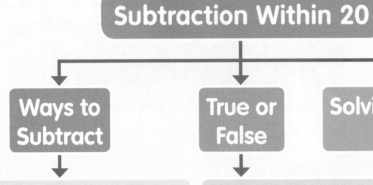

Subtraction Within 20

Ways to Subtract

You can count back from the greater number to subtract.
17 − 3 = 14

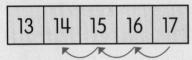

13	14	15	16	17

You can group into a 10 and ones to subtract.

12 − 4 = 8

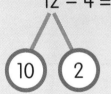

You can use addition facts to help you subtract.

14 − 5 = ?
5 + 9 = 14 is the related addition fact.
So, 14 − 5 = 9.

True or False

You can check if a number sentence is true or false.
5 + 6 = 13 − 2 is true.
11 − 2 = 14 − 6 is false.

Solving Real-World Problems

Kate has 18 beads.
She gives Caleb 9 beads.
How many beads does Kate have left?

18 − 9 = 9
Kate has 9 beads left.

Name: _____ Date: _____

Add.
Count on from the greater number.
Draw arrows to help you.

1 12 + 3 = _____ | 12 | 13 | 14 | 15 | 16 |

2 16 + 4 = _____ | 16 | 17 | 18 | 19 | 20 |

Make a 10.
Then, add.

3   9 + 7 = _____   **4**   7 + 8 = _____

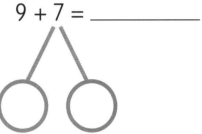

Circle the correct answer.

5 Which is a doubles fact?

4 + 5 = 9   6 + 6 = 12   8 + 2 = 10

6 Which is a doubles plus one fact?

4 + 4 = 8   14 + 1 = 15   5 + 6 = 11

Add.

7 8 + 4 = _____   **8** 6 + 7 = _____

Subtract.
Count back from the greater number.
Draw arrows to help you.

9 14 − 2 = _____

11	12	13	14

10 18 − 3 = _____

14	15	16	17	18

Group each number into a 10 and ones.
Then, subtract.

11 12 − 6 = _____

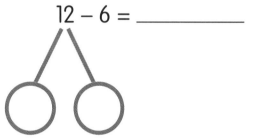

12 14 − 8 = _____

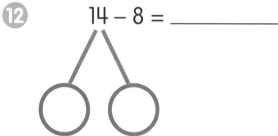

Make a fact family for the number sentence.

13 8 + 9 = _____   _____ − _____ = _____

_____ + _____ = _____   _____ − _____ = _____

Subtract.
Use a related addition fact to help you.
Write the related addition fact.

14 12 − 9 = _____

Addition fact: _____ + _____ = 12

15 _____ − 6 = 9

Addition fact: _____ + _____ = _____

Look at each number sentence.
Is it true or false?
Add or subtract to find out.
Then, circle true or false.

16 7 + 6 = 16 − 9

7 + 6 = _____   16 − 9 = _____

This number sentence is   true   /   false   .

17 11 + 4 = 7 + 8

11 + 4 = _____   7 + 8 = _____

This number sentence is   true   /   false   .

Solve.

18 A store sells 9 hats in the morning.
It sells 5 hats in the afternoon.
How many hats does the store sell in all?

_____ ◯ _____ = _____

The store sells _____ hats in all.

19 There are 14 glasses of juice at a party.
The guests drink some juice.
There are 7 glasses of juice left.
How many glasses of juice do the guests drink?

_____ ◯ _____ = _____

The guests drink _____ glasses of juice.

Assessment Prep
Answer each question.

20 Which number sentence is false?

Ⓐ 16 + 2 = 18

Ⓑ 20 − 2 = 18

Ⓒ 9 + 9 = 18

Ⓓ 20 − 3 = 18

21 Which boxes give an answer that is less than 6?
Color them.

12 − 8	13 − 7	14 − 6	11 − 7

Walking Along a Beach

1 Madelyn finds 7 seashells on the beach.
Yong finds 3 more seashells than Madelyn.

a How many seashells does Yong find?

_____ ◯ _____ = _____

Yong finds _____ seashells.

b How many seashells do the children find in all?

_____ ◯ _____ = _____

The children find _____ seashells in all.

2 Complete the number sentence.
Use the pictures to help you.

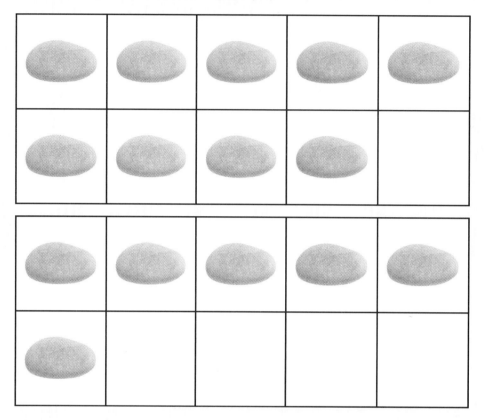

9 + _____ = _____

Write how you know.

3 Naomi writes these number sentences on the sand.

a Fill in each missing number.

_____ – 9 = 5

9 + 5 = _____

b What does "=" mean?

4 Mr. Taylor catches 13 crabs.
Some crabs are in the pail.
How many crabs are in the pail?

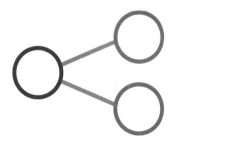

_____ ○ _____ = _____

There are _____ crabs in the pail.

Rubric

Point(s)	Level	My Performance
7–8	4	• Most of my answers are correct. • I show all my work correctly. • I explain my thinking clearly and completely.
5–6.5	3	• Some of my answers are correct. • I show some of my work correctly. • I explain my thinking clearly.
3–4.5	2	• A few of my answers are correct. • I show little work correctly. • I explain some of my thinking clearly.
0–2.5	1	• A few of my answers are correct. • I show little or no work. • I do not explain my thinking clearly.

Teacher's Comments

Hula-Hoop Garden

Lots of things live in a garden.
There are plants.
There are animals and insects too.
What can you see in a garden?

Task

Make addition and subtraction stories

Work in pairs.

1. Take a walk with your class.
   Carry a hula-hoop with you.

2. Put your hula-hoop on the grass or in the flowerbed.
   Then, look for living things inside the hoop.

3. Count what you see.
   Draw what you count.

4. Write an addition story for your picture.

5. Write a subtraction story for your picture.

6. Share your stories with your class.

Numbers to 40

How can you keep track of a large number of objects?
How can you use place value to help you?

Name: _____ Date: _____

Counting on from 10 to 20

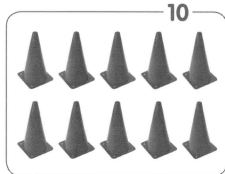

10, 11, 12, 13, 14, 15, 16, 17

There are 17 .

17 in words is seventeen.

▶ **Quick Check**

**Count on from 10.
Then, write the number and word.**

1 How many ⎯ are there?

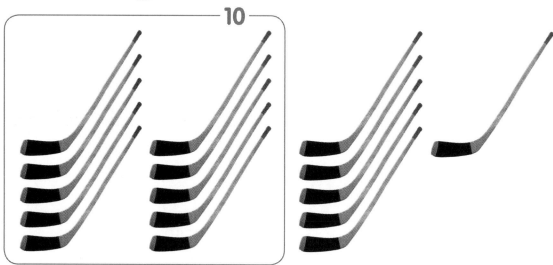

Write the number. _____

Write the word. _____

Count on.
Then, write each missing number.

2

1	2	3			6	7	8	9	
11		13				17	18	19	

Making a 10, and then counting on

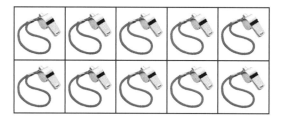

10 and 5 make 15.
10 + 5 = 15

▶ Quick Check

Fill in each blank.

3 10 and 8 make _____.

4 10 + 8 = _____

Reading place-value charts

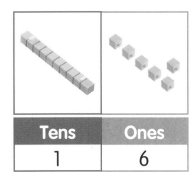

Tens	Ones
1	6

1 ten 6 ones is the same as 16 ones.

16 is 1 ten 6 ones.
16 = 10 + 6

▶ **Quick Check**

Write each missing number.

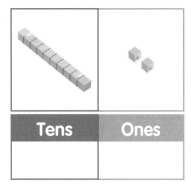

Tens	Ones

12 is _____ ten _____ ones

12 = _____ + 2

6 20 is _____ tens _____ ones

20 = _____ + 0

Comparing and ordering numbers

Compare 14, 12, and 20.

Tens	Ones
1	4
1	2
2	0

Step 1
Compare the tens.
2 tens are greater than 1 ten.
20 is the greatest number.

Step 2
Compare the ones.
4 ones are greater than 2 ones.
So, 14 is greater than 12.
12 is the least number.

Order the numbers from greatest to least.
20, 14, 12

Order the numbers from least to greatest.
12, 14, 20

▶ **Quick Check**

**Compare and order the numbers.
Then, fill in each blank.**

 12   2   20

7 _____ is greater than 12.

8 _____ is less than 12.

9 _____ is the greatest number.

10 _____ is the least number.

Order the numbers from greatest to least.

_____, _____, _____
greatest   least

Order the numbers from least to greatest.

19   9   11

_____, _____, _____
least   greatest

Number patterns

12, 14, 16, 18, ?
The numbers are arranged in a pattern.
Each number is 2 more than the number before it.
The next number is 2 more than 18.
It is 20.

▶ Quick Check

Write the missing numbers in each number pattern.

13 9, 10, 11, 12, _____, _____, _____, 16

14 20, _____, 16, _____, 12, 10, 8, 6

Counting to 40

Learning Objectives:
- Count on from 20 to 40.
- Read and write 21 to 40 in numbers and words.

New Vocabulary

twenty-one	twenty-two
twenty-three	twenty-four
twenty-five	twenty-six
twenty-seven	twenty-eight
twenty-nine	thirty
forty	

THINK

Count and write the number of  in each group.

_____   _____   _____   _____

What is the fastest way to find the number of 🔲 in all?
Why do you think so?

ENGAGE

a   Take a bag of 🔵.
Pour them on the table.
How many 🔵 are there?
What is a quick way to count them?
Talk about how you count with your partner.

b   Will you use the same way to count the 🔵 again?
Why?

LEARN Count to 40

① You can count on by ones.

1, 2, 3, 4, 5, 6, 7, 8, 9, 10

11, 12, 13, 14, 15, 16, 17, 18, 19, 20, 21, 22

You can also make tens.
Then, count on by tens and ones.

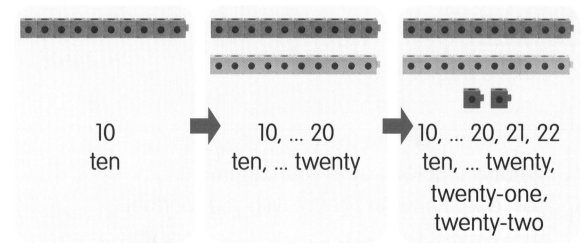

| 10 ten | 10, ... 20 ten, ... twenty | 10, ... 20, 21, 22 ten, ... twenty, twenty-one, twenty-two |

There are 22 .

2 You can count on by tens and ones.

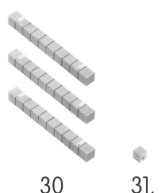

ten, …, twenty, …, thirty, thirty-one, thirty-two, thirty-three, thirty-four

30   31,   32,   33,   34

There are 34 .

3 You can count on by tens.

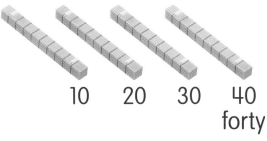

10   20   30   40
                    forty

ten, …, twenty, …, thirty, …, forty

10, 20, 30, 40
They are 40 .

Hands-on Activity Counting to 40

Work in pairs.

Your teacher will give you a bag of .

① Ask your partner to take some from the bag.

② Count the that your partner has taken.
Talk about how you count with him or her.

③ Trade places.
Repeat ① and ②.

TRY Practice counting to 40

Count on by tens and ones.
Then, fill in each blank.

1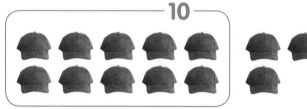

10, …, 20, _____, _____, _____

Count on by tens and ones.
Then, write each number and word.

		Number	Word
2	(2 rods and 4 cubes)	_____	_____
3	(3 rods and 9 cubes)	_____	_____

Show the number.
Draw ▭ for tens and □ for ones.

	Number	
4	22	
5	34	

INDEPENDENT PRACTICE

Count on by tens and ones.
Then, fill in each blank.

1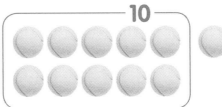

10, …, 20, _____, _____, _____, _____, _____

2

10, …, 20, …, _____, _____, _____, _____

3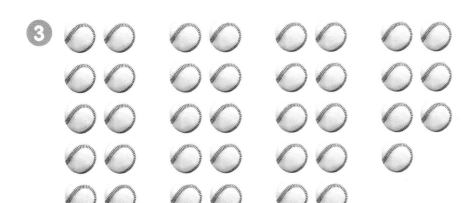

10, …, _____, …, _____, _____, _____, _____,

_____, _____, _____, _____

Make groups of 10.
Then, count on and write the number.

④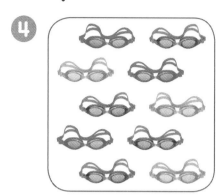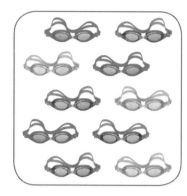

_____

⑤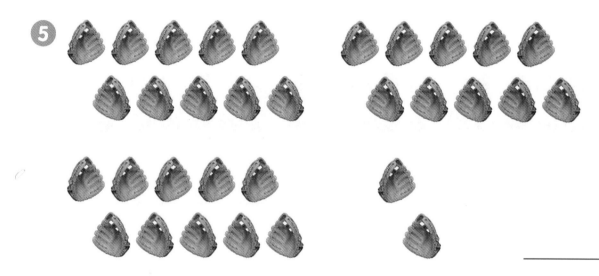

_____

⑥

_____

Draw lines to match the 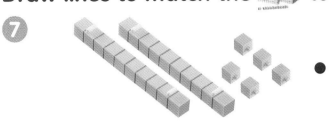 **to its number.**

7

●

● forty

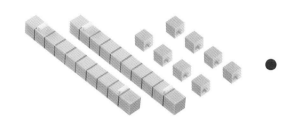
●

● twenty-five

●

● twenty-eight

●

● thirty-six

Count the .
Then, write each number and word.

8
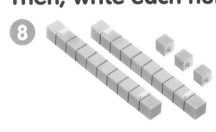

Number ＿＿＿＿＿

Word ＿＿＿＿＿

9

Number _____

Word _____

10

Number _____

Word _____

11

Number _____

Word _____

Write each number.

12 twenty-nine _____

13 thirty-eight _____

Write each word.

14 21 _____

15 35 _____

Place Value

Learning Objectives:
- Use a place-value chart to show numbers to 40.
- Use tens and ones to show numbers to 40.

THINK

Look at each place-value chart.
What number does each place-value chart show?
Write each number.

1

Tens	Ones
2	12

= _____

2

Tens	Ones
	38

= _____

Talk about your answers with your partner.

ENGAGE

1 Show 2 tens 3 ones and 3 tens 2 ones on a place-value chart.
Are they the same or different?
Why do you think so?

2 Use  to show 35 in three different ways.
Ask your partner to tell why they are the same.

1

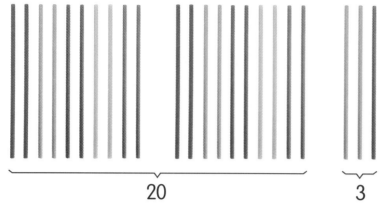

20   3

20 and 3 make 23.
So, 20 + 3 = 23.

23 = 2 tens 3 ones
23 = 20 + 3

Tens	Ones
2	3

2

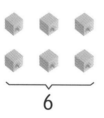

30   6

30 and 6 make 36.
So, 30 + 6 = 36.

36 = 3 tens 6 ones
36 = 30 + 6

Tens	Ones
3	6

Math Talk

There are 38 students at the gym.
Tell your partner how you use to show the number of students.

Take 40 ▊▊▊▊.

① Show 22 in tens and ones.

You can bundle each group of 10 ▊▊▊▊ together.

② **Mathematical Habit 7** **Make use of structure**

Write 22 on the place-value chart.

Tens	Ones

③ Repeat ① and ② for these numbers.

27
Tens	Ones

30
Tens	Ones

33
Tens	Ones

34
Tens	Ones

35
Tens	Ones

40
Tens	Ones

TRY Practice using place value to show numbers to 40

Count on by tens and ones.
Then, write each missing number.

1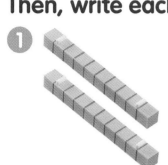

20 and 8 make ____.
So, 20 + 8 = ____.

Tens	Ones

28 = _____ tens _____ ones

2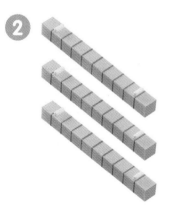

30 and 7 make ____.
So, 30 + 7 = ____.

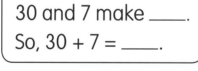

Tens	Ones

37 = _____ tens _____ ones

3 30 = _____ tens _____ ones

Tens	Ones

INDEPENDENT PRACTICE

Count on by tens and ones.
Then, fill in each blank.

1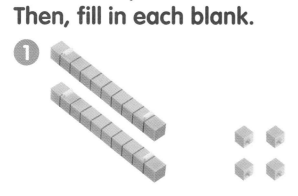

24 = _____ tens _____ ones

Tens	Ones

2

32 = _____ tens _____ ones

Tens	Ones

Color to show the correct number of tens and ones.
Then, write each missing number.

3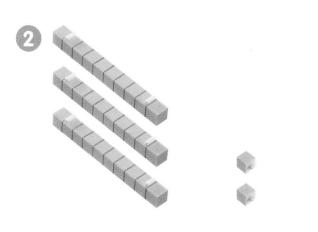

25 = _____ tens _____ ones

Tens	Ones

4

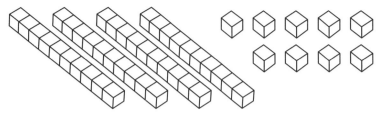

39 = _____ tens _____ ones

Tens	Ones

Write each missing number.

5 27 = _____ tens _____ ones

6 35 = _____ tens _____ ones

7 40 = _____ tens _____ ones

Which is the odd one out?
Make an X.

8

| twenty-six | 2 tens 6 ones | 25 | 20 + 6 |

9

| 31 | 30 + 1 | thirty-one | 3 tens |

10

| 30 + 4 | thirty-three | 3 tens 3 ones | 33 |

3 Comparing, Ordering, and Number Patterns

Learning Objectives:
- Use a strategy to compare numbers to 40.
- Order numbers to 40.
- Find the missing numbers in a number pattern.

THINK

Santino has five cards.
Each card has a number.
He wants to make a number pattern.
Two numbers are covered up.
What do you think the numbers are?
Share your thinking with your partner.

ENGAGE

a   Take 8  and 16 .

Regroup each color into a ten and ones.

Are there more or ?

b   Move from one group to the other to show the same number.

How many did you move?

How many are there in each group now?

LEARN Compare sets and numbers

1

Set A  12

Set B  8

12 is greater than 8.
8 is less than 12.

12 − 8 = 4

Set A has 4 more pears than Set B.
Set B has 4 fewer pears than Set A.

How do you subtract 8 from 12?

Hands-on Activity Comparing sets and numbers

Your teacher will give you two bags of 🔵.

① Take some 🔵 from each bag.

② Arrange the 🔵 to show which color has more.

Which color has more? _____

How many more? _____

③ Repeat ① and ②.

© 2020 Marshall Cavendish Education Pte Ltd

TRY Practice comparing sets and numbers

Count and compare.
Then, fill in each blank.

Set A

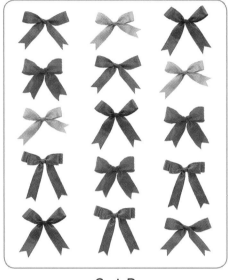

Set B

1. Set A has _____ bows.

2. Set B has _____ bows.

3. Which set has more? _____

4. How many more? _____

5. Which set has fewer? _____

6. How many fewer? _____

7. _____ is greater than _____.

8. _____ is less than _____.

ENGAGE

Use a counting tape to help you.

1 Daniel has 24 cards.
Kaylee has 2 more cards than Daniel.
Zane has 3 fewer cards than Daniel.
How many cards does each person have?

2 Fill in each blank.

a ___ more than 27 is 35.   b 4 less than ___ is 38.

LEARN Compare numbers using a counting tape

1 Find 2 more than 27.

2 more

26	27	28	29	30

29 is 2 more than 27.
29 is greater than 27.

Count on from 27.

2 Find 2 less than 38.

2 less

31	32	33	34	35	36	37	38	39	40

36 is 2 less than 38.
36 is less than 38.

Count back from 38.

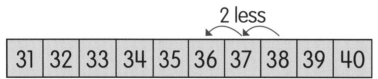

Math Talk

Is it true that you add when you see "more than"?
Is it true that you subtract when you see "less than"?
Share your thinking with your partner.

TRY Practice using a counting tape to compare numbers

Fill in each blank.

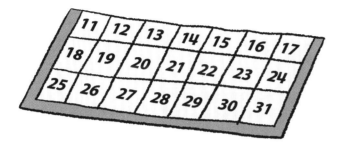

1 _____ is 2 more than 22.

_____ is greater than 22.

Count on from 22.

2 _____ is 3 less than 31.

_____ is less than 31.

Count back from 31.

ENGAGE

a There are 27 students in Mr. Clark's class.
There are 32 students in Ms. Cook's class.
Use 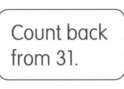 to show the number of students in each class.
Which class has more students?
How do you know?

b Some students joined the class with fewer students.
Now, this class has more students.
What is the least number of students that joined this class?

LEARN Compare numbers with different tens

① Compare 28 and 31.

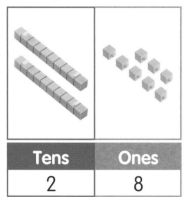

Tens	Ones
2	8

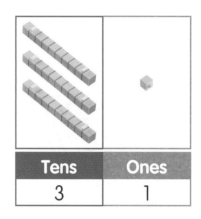

Tens	Ones
3	1

First, compare the tens.
They are different.
3 tens are greater than 2 tens.
So, 31 is greater than 28.
You can write 31 > 28.

">" means greater than.

TRY Practice comparing numbers with different tens

Compare the numbers.
Then, fill in each blank.

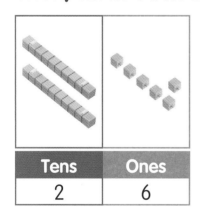

Tens	Ones
2	6

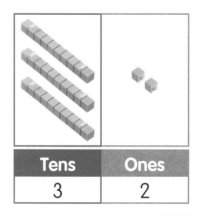

Tens	Ones
3	2

① _____ is greater than _____.

② _____ > _____

Compare the tens.
Are they equal?

ENGAGE

a There are 32 ducks and 38 geese in a pond.
Use 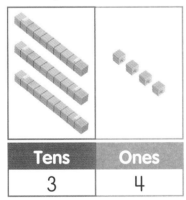 to show the number of ducks and geese.
Are there more geese or ducks?
How do you know?

b There are also some frogs at the pond.
There are as many frogs as the smaller group of animals.
More frogs come to the pond.
Now, the frogs become the largest group of animals.
What is the least number of frogs that came to the pond?

LEARN Compare numbers with equal tens

① Compare 34 and 37.

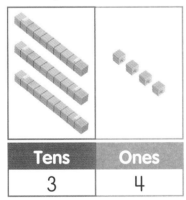

Tens	Ones
3	4

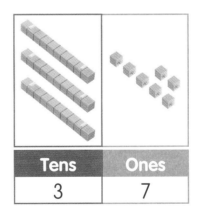

Tens	Ones
3	7

First, compare the tens.
They are the same.
Then, compare the ones.

4 ones are fewer than 7 ones.
So, 34 is less than 37.
You can write 34 < 37.

"<" means less than.

TRY Practice comparing numbers with equal tens

Compare the numbers.
Then, fill in each blank.

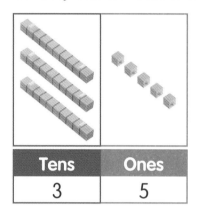

Tens	Ones
3	5

Tens	Ones
3	4

1 _____ is less than _____.

2 _____ < _____

> Compare the tens.
> Then, compare the ones.
> Are they equal?

ENGAGE

a Use [cube] to show 26, 34, and 30.
Which number is the greatest?
Which number is the least?
Share how you find your answers with your partner.

b How can you make the three numbers equal?
Share your thinking with your partner.

LEARN Compare and order three numbers

1 Compare 27, 35, and 33.

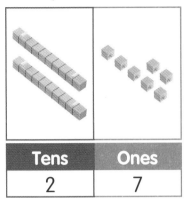

Tens	Ones
2	7

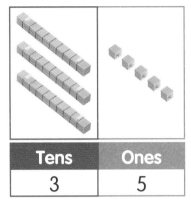

Tens	Ones
3	5

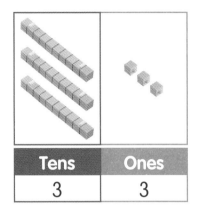

Tens	Ones
3	3

Compare the tens.
They are different.
3 tens are greater than 2 tens.
So, 27 is the least number.

Then, compare the ones.
They are different.
5 ones are greater than 3 ones.
So, 35 is the greatest number.

Order the numbers from greatest to least:

35   33   27

greatest   least

Can you order the numbers from least to greatest?

Hands-on Activity Comparing and ordering three numbers

Work in pairs.

① Use 📦 to show these numbers to your partner.

33   28   36

② Ask your partner to describe the numbers.
Use these helping words.

same   different   greater   less

greatest   least   order

Example:

36 and 33 have the same tens.
36 is greater than 33.

③ Trade places.
Repeat ① and ② for these numbers.

a   36   24   31   b   23   38   27

TRY Practice comparing and ordering three numbers

Compare and order the numbers.
Fill in each blank.

34 29 38

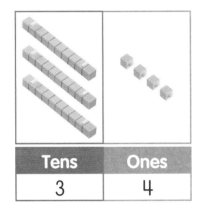

Tens	Ones
3	4

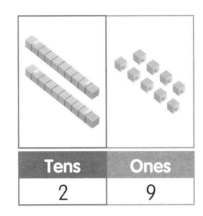

Tens	Ones
2	9

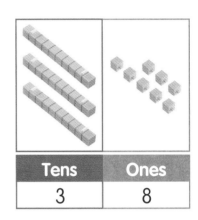

Tens	Ones
3	8

1 _____ is the least number.

2 _____ is the greatest number.

Compare the tens.
2 tens are less than 3 tens.

3 Order the numbers from least to greatest.

_____, _____, _____
least   greatest

ENGAGE

a Look at this number pattern.
20, _____, _____, 29, 32, 35, 38
What do you notice?

b Share a new pattern with your partner.

LEARN Find missing numbers in a number pattern

1

2 more   2 more   2 more

| 19 | 21 | 23 | 25 | ? | 29 | 31 | 33 | 35 | 37 | ? |

2 more than
25 is 27.

2 more than
37 is 39.

I find each number by adding 2
to the number before it.

2

2 less   2 less   2 less

| 20 | 22 | 24 | 26 | ? | 30 | 32 | 34 | 36 | ? | 40 |

2 less than
30 is 28.

2 less than
40 is 38.

I find each number by subtracting 2
from the number after it.

Cartel makes this number pattern.

?	23	25	27	29	?	33

Talk about how you find each missing number with your partner.

TRY Practice finding missing numbers in a number pattern

Write each missing number.

1

____ more than 34 is ____.

____ more than 39 is ____.

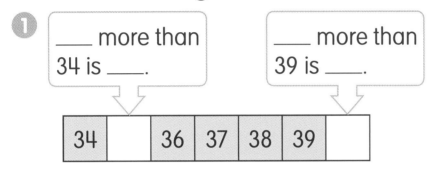

34		36	37	38	39	

2

____ less than 18 is ____.

____ less than 28 is ____.

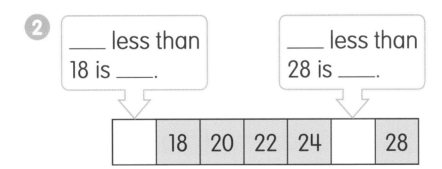

	18	20	22	24		28

3

27			33	35	37	39

These number cards make a number pattern.

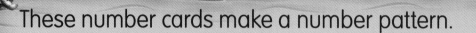

| 27 | 31 | 25 | | 29 | |

1. What can be the numbers on the cards facing down?
Give two answers.

Another seven cards make a number pattern.

| 27 | 19 | | | 23 | | 17 |

2. What can be the numbers on the cards facing down?
Give three answers.

Name: _____ Date: _____

INDEPENDENT PRACTICE 🗒

Count and compare.
Then, fill in each blank.

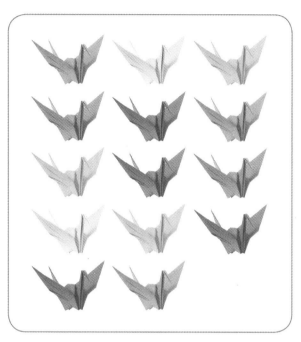

Amari

Faith

1 Amari makes _____ paper cranes.

2 Faith makes _____ paper cranes.

3 Amari makes _____ more paper cranes than Faith.

4 Faith makes _____ fewer paper cranes than Amari.

5 _____ is greater than _____.

6 _____ is less than _____.

Fill in each blank.
Use the counting tape to help you.

27	28	29	30	31	32	33	34	35	36	37	38	39	40

7 _____ is 2 more than 28.

_____ is greater than 28.

8 _____ is 3 less than 40.

_____ is less than 40.

9 3 more than 29 is _____.

_____ is greater than 29.

Color the greater number.

10

Color the number that is less.

11

Fill in each blank with <, >, or =.

12 33 ◯ 40

13 28 ◯ 26

Which sentences describe the numbers?

Color the ⬡▷**.**

14

⭐ 39   ⭐ 27   ⭐ 32

39 is less than 32. ▷

◁ 32 is greater than 27.

39 is the greatest number. ▷

◁ 27 is the least number.

Order the numbers from least to greatest.

15

32   40   23

_____, _____, _____
  least   greatest

Order the numbers from greatest to least.

16

_____, _____, _____
greatest   least

Write the missing numbers in each number pattern.

17

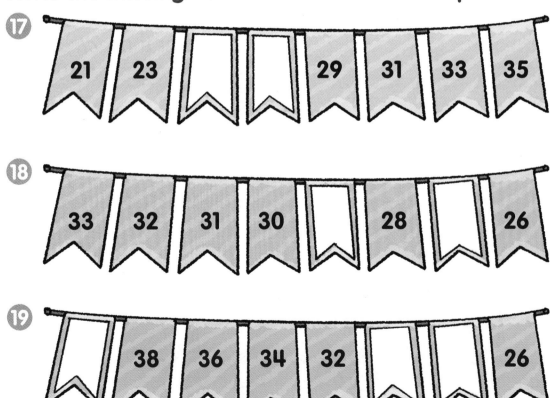

| 21 | 23 | | | 29 | 31 | 33 | 35 |

18

| 33 | 32 | 31 | 30 | | 28 | | 26 |

19

| | 38 | 36 | 34 | 32 | | | 26 |

Name: _____ Date: _____

Mathematical Habit 3 Construct viable arguments

Callia makes a number pattern as shown.

| 28 | 30 | 32 | 34 | 36 | 38 |

Write three sentences about Callia's number pattern.
Use these words to help you.

greater than   less than   greatest

least   more than

add   subtract   count on

count back

Problem Solving with Heuristics

1 **Mathematical Habit** **1** Persevere in solving problems

You have three numbers, A , B , and C .

A is greater than 21 but less than 26.

B is greater than 26 but less than 32.

B is 3 more than A but 3 less than C .

C is greater than 30.

What is B ?

Write down all the likely numbers for A, B, and C.

② **Mathematical Habit 1** Persevere in solving problems

Kayla makes a number pattern with six of the following cards.

Which two cards does Kayla **not** use?

| 27 | 31 | 23 | 37 | 33 | 25 | 36 | 29 |

CHAPTER WRAP-UP

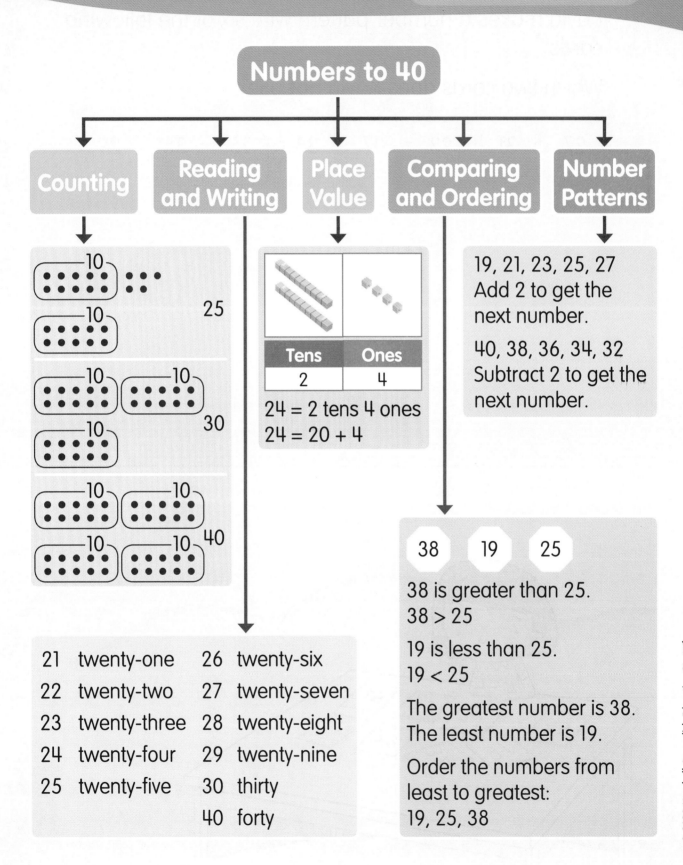

Numbers to 40

Counting

10 ••• 25

10

10   10

10   30

10   10

10   10 40

Reading and Writing

21	twenty-one	26	twenty-six
22	twenty-two	27	twenty-seven
23	twenty-three	28	twenty-eight
24	twenty-four	29	twenty-nine
25	twenty-five	30	thirty
		40	forty

Place Value

Tens	Ones
2	4

24 = 2 tens 4 ones
24 = 20 + 4

Comparing and Ordering

38   19   25

38 is greater than 25.
38 > 25

19 is less than 25.
19 < 25

The greatest number is 38.
The least number is 19.

Order the numbers from least to greatest:
19, 25, 38

Number Patterns

19, 21, 23, 25, 27
Add 2 to get the next number.

40, 38, 36, 34, 32
Subtract 2 to get the next number.

Name: _____   Date: _____

Count on by tens and ones.
Then, write each number and word.

1

Number _____   Word _____

2

Number _____   Word _____

3
 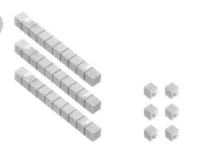

Number _____   Word _____

Make groups of 10.
Then, count on and write the number.

4

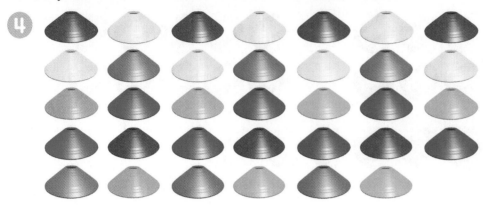

_____

Count on by tens and ones.
Then, fill in each blank.

5

Tens	Ones

23 = _____ tens _____ ones

6

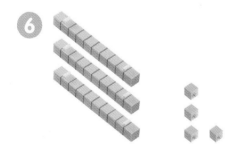

Tens	Ones

34 = _____ tens _____ ones

Fill in each blank.

7 2 tens 5 ones = _____

8 29 = _____ tens _____ ones

Count and compare.
Then, answer each question.

Mario

Ashley

9 Mario paints _____ flowers.

10 Ashley paints _____ flowers.

11 Who paints fewer flowers? _____

12 How many fewer? _____

13 _____ is less than _____.

Fill in each blank.
Use the counting tape to help you.

27	28	29	30	31	32	33	34	35	36	37	38	39	40

⑭ _____ is 2 more than 30.

⑮ _____ is 2 less than 31.

⑯ 3 more than 37 is _____.

⑰ 3 less than 30 is _____.

Compare the numbers.
Then, fill in each blank.

⑱   29   34

_____ is greater than _____.

_____ > _____

⑲   32   39

_____ is less than _____.

_____ < _____

Order the numbers from greatest to least.

20 22 29 27

_____ , _____ , _____
greatest   least

Order the numbers from least to greatest.

21 24 34 32

_____ , _____ , _____
least   greatest

Write the missing numbers in each number pattern.

22 18 19 20 21 ___ 23 ___ ___

23 38 ___ 36 35 34 33 ___ ___

24 ___ ___ 26 ___ 22 20 18 16

Assessment Prep
Answer each question.

25 Compare the numbers.
Which sentences describe the numbers correctly?
Color the boxes.

| 27 | 31 | 24 |

27 is 4 less than 31.	27 is 3 more than 24.
4 more than 31 is 27.	3 more than 24 is 31.

26 The five cards make a number pattern.
Which are the two numbers on the cards facing down?

Color the ☁.

26   24   28

22, 30   23, 29

22, 25   25, 27

Name: _____   Date: _____

Sports Store

1 Ethan finds some soccer balls in the sports store.
There are numbers on them.

21   32   37   34   28   20

a   _____ is greater than _____.

b   _____ is 2 less than 34.

c   The numbers on the balls are ordered from least to greatest.
Write each missing number.

21   28   32   34

least   greatest

2 Audrey counts the baseballs in the store.

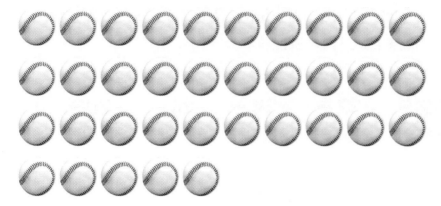

_____ = _____ tens _____ ones

3 These footballs are arranged to make a pattern.

a Write the missing numbers in the number pattern.

b Write how you find the number pattern.

4 Each basketball has a number on it.
Ang chooses a basketball.
Which basketball does Ang choose?
Use these clues to help you.

> **Clues**
> The number on the basketball is less than 35.
> It has a 3 in the tens place.
> It is greater than 32.

Which basketball matches the clues?
Make an ✘ on the basketballs that do not match.
Circle the basketball that matches.

Rubric

Point(s)	Level	My Performance
7–8	4	• Most of my answers are correct. • I show all my work correctly. • I explain my thinking clearly and completely.
5–6.5	3	• Some of my answers are correct. • I show some of my work correctly. • I explain my thinking clearly.
3–4.5	2	• A few of my answers are correct. • I show little work correctly. • I explain some of my thinking clearly.
0–2.5	1	• A few of my answers are correct. • I show little or no work. • I do not explain my thinking clearly.

Teacher's Comments

What do you do at different times of the day?

Name: _____   Date: _____

Using ordinal numbers and position

The children are running in a race.
Trevon came in first.
Lilian came in third.
Rafaela came in eighth.
Emily was last.

▶ Quick Check

Ten children are running in a race.

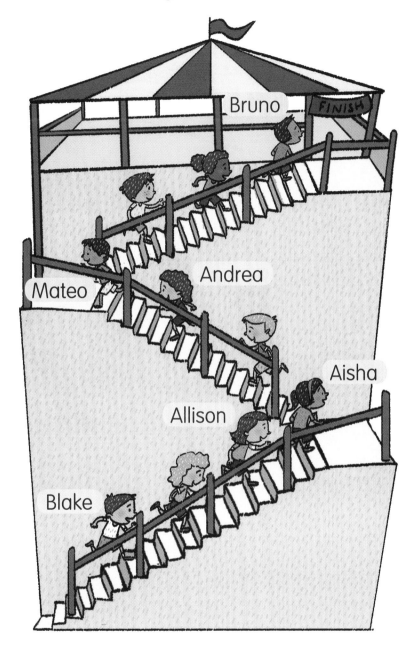

Fill in each blank.

1 _____ is fourth.

2 _____ is last.

3 _____ is 7th.

Ten children are taking part in a bicycle race.

Fill in each blank.

4 _____ is first in the race.

5 _____ is in the fifth position.

6 _____ is eighth in the race.

7 Jazmin is _____ in the race.

8 Henry is _____ in the race.

Using a Calendar

Learning Objectives:
- Read a calendar.
- Know the days of the week.
- Know the months of the year.
- Write the date.
- Know the seasons of the year.

New Vocabulary

calendar	days
weeks	months
year	date
seasons	warmer
colder	

THINK

FEBRUARY						
Sun.	Mon.	Tue.	Wed.	Thu.	Fri.	Sat.
				1	2	3
4	5	6	7	8	9	10
11	12	13	14	15	16	17
18	19	20	21	22	23	24
25	26	27	28			

Dominic's birthday is on February 21.
February 21 falls on a Wednesday.
Ayden's birthday is 25 days after Dominic's birthday.

a   What is the date of Ayden's birthday?

b   Which day does Ayden's birthday fall on?

Take a calendar.
Flip through the calendar.
Look at the number of days and weeks of each month.
Talk about what pattern you see with your partner.

LEARN Know the calendar and the days of the week

Each of these is a calendar.
A calendar shows the days, weeks, and months of a year.

There are seven days in one week.
The first day of the week is Sunday.
The last day of the week is Saturday.

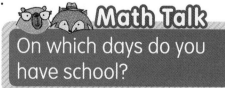

Math Talk
On which days do you have school?

③ You can write the days of the week in short form.

Sunday ⟶ Sun.

Monday ⟶ Mon.

Tuesday ⟶ Tue.

Wednesday ⟶ Wed.

Thursday ⟶ Thu.

Friday ⟶ Fri.

Saturday ⟶ Sat.

Hands-on Activity Ordering the days of the week

Work in pairs.

① Write each day of the week on small cards.

② Point and read the names of the days to your partner.

③ Mix the cards.
Then, ask your partner to put them in order.

④ Trade places.
Repeat ③.

TRY Practice identifying the days of the week

Fill in each blank.

1. There are _____ days in a week.

2. _____ is the first day of the week.

3. The last day of the week is _____.

4. _____ comes right before Tuesday.

5. _____ is the day between Tuesday and Thursday.

6. _____ is the day that comes right after Thursday.

7. _____ is the third day of the week.

8. _____ is the sixth day of the week.

ENGAGE

1. Look at a calendar.
   What are the months of the year?
   Which months have 30 days?
   Which months have 31 days?

2. Use the knuckles and grooves on your fists and say the months.
   What pattern do you notice?

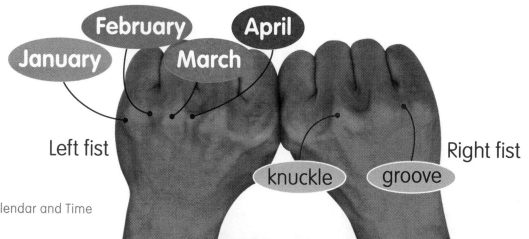

January   February   March   April

Left fist   Right fist

knuckle   groove

LEARN Know the months of the year

JANUARY

Sun.	Mon.	Tue.	Wed.	Thu.	Fri.	Sat.
					1	2
3	4	5	6	7	8	9
10	11	12	13	14	15	16
17	18	19	20	21	22	23
24	25	26	27	28	29	30
31						

FEBRUARY

Sun.	Mon.	Tue.	Wed.	Thu.	Fri.	Sat.
	1	2	3	4	5	6
7	8	9	10	11	12	13
14	15	16	17	18	19	20
21	22	23	24	25	26	27
28						

MARCH

Sun.	Mon.	Tue.	Wed.	Thu.	Fri.	Sat.
	1	2	3	4	5	6
7	8	9	10	11	12	13
14	15	16	17	18	19	20
21	22	23	24	25	26	27
28	29	30	31			

APRIL

Sun.	Mon.	Tue.	Wed.	Thu.	Fri.	Sat.
				1	2	3
4	5	6	7	8	9	10
11	12	13	14	15	16	17
18	19	20	21	22	23	24
25	26	27	28	29	30	

MAY

Sun.	Mon.	Tue.	Wed.	Thu.	Fri.	Sat.
						1
2	3	4	5	6	7	8
9	10	11	12	13	14	15
16	17	18	19	20	21	22
23	24	25	26	27	28	29
30	31					

JUNE

Sun.	Mon.	Tue.	Wed.	Thu.	Fri.	Sat.
		1	2	3	4	5
6	7	8	9	10	11	12
13	14	15	16	17	18	19
20	21	22	23	24	25	26
27	28	29	30			

JULY

Sun.	Mon.	Tue.	Wed.	Thu.	Fri.	Sat.
				1	2	3
4	5	6	7	8	9	10
11	12	13	14	15	16	17
18	19	20	21	22	23	24
25	26	27	28	29	30	31

AUGUST

Sun.	Mon.	Tue.	Wed.	Thu.	Fri.	Sat.
1	2	3	4	5	6	7
8	9	10	11	12	13	14
15	16	17	18	19	20	21
22	23	24	25	26	27	28
29	30	31				

SEPTEMBER

Sun.	Mon.	Tue.	Wed.	Thu.	Fri.	Sat.
			1	2	3	4
5	6	7	8	9	10	11
12	13	14	15	16	17	18
19	20	21	22	23	24	25
26	27	28	29	30		

OCTOBER

Sun.	Mon.	Tue.	Wed.	Thu.	Fri.	Sat.
					1	2
3	4	5	6	7	8	9
10	11	12	13	14	15	16
17	18	19	20	21	22	23
24	25	26	27	28	29	30
31						

NOVEMBER

Sun.	Mon.	Tue.	Wed.	Thu.	Fri.	Sat.
	1	2	3	4	5	6
7	8	9	10	11	12	13
14	15	16	17	18	19	20
21	22	23	24	25	26	27
28	29	30				

DECEMBER

Sun.	Mon.	Tue.	Wed.	Thu.	Fri.	Sat.
			1	2	3	4
5	6	7	8	9	10	11
12	13	14	15	16	17	18
19	20	21	22	23	24	25
26	27	28	29	30	31	

There are 12 months in one year.
The first month of the year is January.
The second month of the year is February.
The last month of the year is December.

Some months have only 30 days.
Some months have 31 days.
How many days are there in February?

TRY **Practice identifying the months of the year**

Fill in each blank.

1. There are _____ months in one year.

2. _____ is the third month of the year.

3. June is the _____ month of the year.

4. _____ is the month between April and June.

5. _____ comes right before August.

6. _____ is the month right after September.

7. April, June, _____, and _____ have only 30 days.

8. _____, _____, _____, _____, _____, _____, and _____ have 31 days.

9. February has _____ or _____ days.

10. School starts in the month of _____.

ENGAGE

a   Look at the calendar.
    What is the date today?
    How can you find the date 26 days from today?

b   Without looking at the calendar, find the date 17 days from today.

LEARN Write the date with the help of a calendar

1 This calendar shows the month of March in the year 2021.
The month begins on a Monday.
The date is March 1, 2021.
The month ends on a Wednesday.
The date is March 31, 2021.

MARCH 2021

Sun.	Mon.	Tue.	Wed.	Thu.	Fri.	Sat.
	1	2	3	4	5	6
7	8	9	10	11	12	13
14	15	16	17	18	19	20
21	22	23	24	25	26	27
28	29	30	31			

Hands-on Activity Using a calendar to find dates

1 Take a calendar.
Circle a date on the calendar.

2 a What is the date 17 days later? _____

b What was the date 17 days earlier? _____

c What is the date 38 days later? _____

d What was the date 38 days earlier? _____

Talk about how you find these dates with your partner.

TRY Practice writing dates with the help of a calendar

Fill in each blank.
Use the calendar to help you.

NOVEMBER 2021

Sun.	Mon.	Tue.	Wed.	Thu.	Fri.	Sat.
	1	2	3	4	5	6
7	8	9	10	11	12	13
14	15	16	17	18	19	20
21	22	23	24	25	26	27
28	29	30				

1. The second day of the month falls on a _____.

2. There are _____ Fridays in November 2021.

3. The date of the first Sunday of the month is _____.

4. If today is the last Wednesday of the month,

   the date is _____.

5. The first day of the next month falls on a _____.

6. A year after November 10, 2021 will be

   November 10, _____.

ENGAGE

a   What is the season now?
    Which month is it now?

b   What is the next season?
    Which month does it begin?
    How many month(s) is it away from now?

LEARN Know the months and seasons of the year

① These are the 12 months in a year.

January	February	March	April
May	June	July	August
September	October	November	December

Months help us to know the seasons of the year.

The Four Seasons

spring

summer

winter

fall

There are four seasons in a year.
They are spring, summer, fall, and winter.
Some months are warmer.
Some months are colder.

Hands-on Activity Making your own calendar

① Make your own calendar.
Show special days.
Birthdays or holidays are some special days.

Year:		Month:				
Sun.	Mon.	Tue.	Wed.	Thu.	Fri.	Sat.

② Which season is your month in? _____

TRY Practice identifying the months and seasons of the year

Fill in each blank.

① _____ comes right before June.

② _____ comes right before winter.

③ Summer comes right after _____.

Answer the question.

④ Ariana was born in spring.
She was born a month before summer.

Which month was Ariana born in? _____

2 Telling Time to the Hour

Learning Objectives:
- Use the term "o'clock" to tell time to the hour.
- Read and tell time to the hour on an analog clock.
- Read and tell time to the hour on a digital clock.

New Vocabulary
o'clock
minute hand
hour hand
digital clock

 **THINK**

Felipe looks at his watch.
One hand points between 4 and 5.
The other hand points between 10 and 11.
What is a possible time to the hour?
Write this hour on the digital clock.

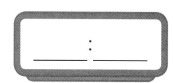

ENGAGE

a   What are the missing numbers on the clock?

b   What time does the clock show?
    Share with your partner how you tell the time.
    Use the positions of the short and long hands on 🕐 to help you.

c   Ask your partner to show 9 o'clock on 🕐.

LEARN Tell time to the hour

1 You can tell time to the hour.

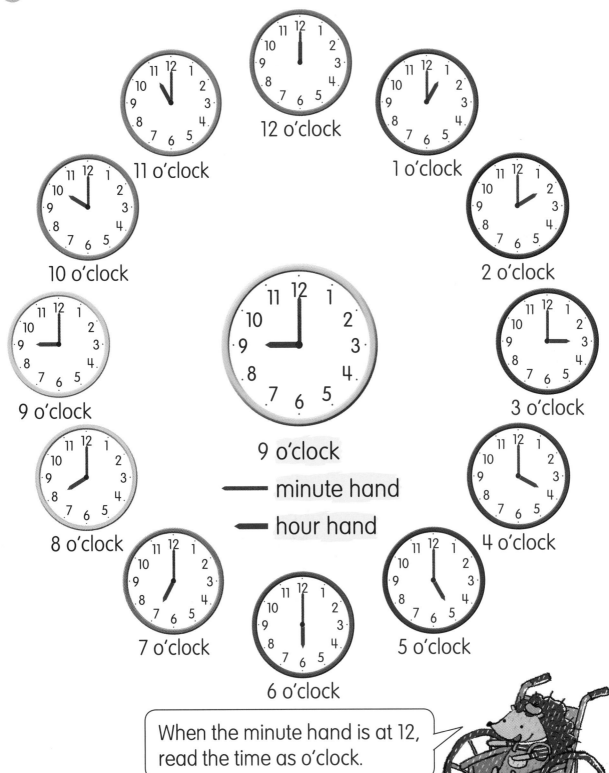

11 o'clock

12 o'clock

1 o'clock

10 o'clock

2 o'clock

9 o'clock

9 o'clock

— minute hand

— hour hand

3 o'clock

8 o'clock

4 o'clock

7 o'clock

6 o'clock

5 o'clock

When the minute hand is at 12, read the time as o'clock.

Math Talk

Hunter says it is 12 o'clock.
Eva says it is 5 o'clock.
Who is correct?
Share what you think with your classmates.

TRY Practice writing time to the hour

Write each time.

1

_____

2

_____

3

_____

4

_____

5

_____

6

_____

ENGAGE

1 The digital clock shows 2:00.
It is 2 o'clock.
Write the time shown on the digital clock at 7 o'clock.

2 Alexa goes to bed at 10 o'clock.
The digital clock in her room is 1 hour slow.
Write the time shown on the digital clock.

LEARN Tell time to the hour on a digital clock

1

hour   minute

12:00

12 o'clock

When the minutes are 00, read the time as o'clock.

3:00

The hour is 3, and the minutes are 00.

The time is 3 o'clock.

Hands-on Activity Making your own clock

① Use these objects to make your own clock.

paper plate

fastener

clock hands

Write the hours on your clock.

② Use your clock to show `8:00`.

③ Say what you do at this time.

④ Repeat ② and ③ for these times.

 `2:00`    `5:00`    `9:00`   `12:00`

TRY Practice writing time to the hour on a digital clock

Write each time.

①

_____ : _____

②

_____ : _____

Write the time to show when you do each activity.

3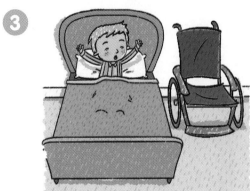

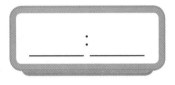 _____ : _____   _____ o'clock

4

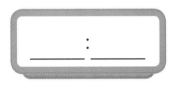 _____ : _____   _____ o'clock

5

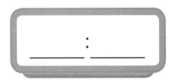 _____ : _____   _____ o'clock

6

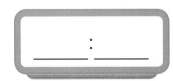 _____ : _____   _____ o'clock

3 Telling Time to the Half Hour

Learning Objectives:
- Use the term "half past" to tell time to the half hour.
- Read and tell time to the half hour on an analog clock.
- Read and tell time to the half hour on a digital clock.

New Vocabulary
half hour
half past

THINK

a Hugo has his lesson at half past 11.
Use 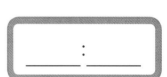 to show the time.
Then, write this time on the digital clock.

b Hugo then has his lunch half an hour later.
Use  to show the time he has lunch.
Then, write this time on the digital clock.

ENGAGE

Adam is going to the movies.

Oh no!
I am half an hour late.

Use 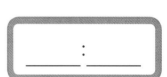 to show the time the movie starts.
How do you know?
Share your thinking with your partner.

LEARN Tell time to the half hour

1

Carson wakes up at 7 o'clock in the morning.

Carson has breakfast at half past 7.

When the minute hand is at 6, it is half past the hour.

The hour hand moves too.

Fill in each blank.
Use the clocks to help you.

Colton feeds his cat at
_____ in the morning.

The children play at _____
in the afternoon.

Malena reads a story at
_____ at night.

Fill in each blank.
Use the clocks to help you.

④

Kwan and Claire go to the fair at _____.

⑤

At _____,
Kwan plays a game.

⑥

At _____, Kwan and Claire take a ride on the Ferris Wheel.

⑦

At _____, Kwan and Claire take a ride on the carousel.

ENGAGE

a   Payton's watch shows half past 7.
    Write this time on the digital clock.

____ : ____

b   One hour earlier, Payton finished reading
    a book.
    Write this time on the digital clock.

____ : ____

c   Payton's watch is half an hour fast.
    Write the correct time she finished reading
    the book.

____ : ____

LEARN Tell time to the half hour on a digital clock

1

hour   minute

12:30

Half past 12

When the minutes
are 30, read the
time as half past
the hour.

3:30

The hour is 3, and
the minutes are 30.

The time is
half past 3.

TRY Practice writing time to the half hour on a digital clock

Fill in each blank.

1

Half past _____

The hour is _____.

The minutes are _____.

2

Half past _____

The hour is _____.

The minutes are _____.

3

Half past _____

_____ : _____

4

Half past _____

_____ : _____

Name: _____ Date: _____

Mathematical Habit 4 Use mathematical models

Write about what you do at different times of the day.
Use **o'clock** and **half past** in your sentences.

What I do in the morning …

What I do in the afternoon …

What I do at night …

Problem Solving with Heuristics

1 **Mathematical Habit** **1** **Persevere in solving problems**

Think of a time to the hour.
At what time of the day or night will the minute hand and the hour hand be on top of each other?
Draw a picture to help you.

2 **Mathematical Habit** **1** **Persevere in solving problems**

Read the clue below.
Then, fill in the dates for May.

Clue
May 8 falls on a Tuesday.

MAY						
Sun.	**Mon.**	**Tue.**	**Wed.**	**Thu.**	**Fri.**	**Sat.**

What is the date of the first Tuesday in June?

_____

How many days are there in May?

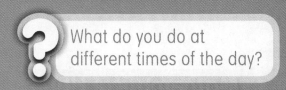

What do you do at different times of the day?

Calendar and Time

```
Calendar and Time
├── Calendar
└── Time
```

Calendar

Days of the week:

Sunday	Monday
Tuesday	Wednesday
Thursday	Friday
Saturday	

Months of the year:

January	February
March	April
May	June
July	August
September	October
November	December

Seasons of the year:

Spring	Summer
Fall	Winter

Time

Read and tell time to the hour.

2 o'clock

Read and tell time to the half hour.

half past 5

Glossary

A

- **alike**

These are red squares. They are alike.

- **as many as**

There are as many rabbits as carrots.

C

- **calendar**

- **colder**

D

- **date**

The date for Fourth of July celebration in 2020 is Saturday, July 4, 2020.

- **days**

There are seven days in one week.

They are Sunday, Monday, Tuesday, Wednesday, Thursday, Friday, and Saturday.

- **different**

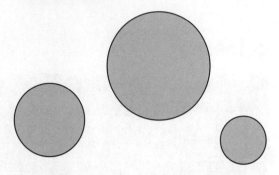

These shapes are circles.
They have different sizes.

- **digital clock**

It is a clock that shows time in digital form.

- **divide**

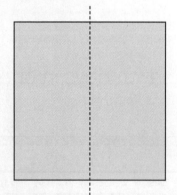

Divide a square into two equal parts.

- **doubles fact**

$3 + 3 = 6$
The numbers that are added are the same.

- **doubles plus one fact**

$4 + 5 = 9$
$4 + 5$ is $4 + 4$ plus one more.

F

- **fact family**

A group of addition and subtraction sentences that have the same parts and whole

$8 + 5 = 13$	$13 - 5 = 8$
$5 + 8 = 13$	$13 - 8 = 5$

- **false**

$5 + 4 = 10$ is a false number sentence.

- **fourths**

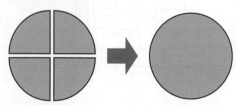

4 fourths make a whole.

fourth of

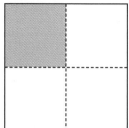

One fourth of the square is shaded.

fewer

There are fewer horses than cows.

forty

Count	Number	Word
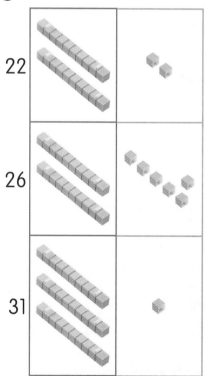	40	forty

G

greater than (>)

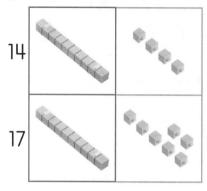

17 is greater than 14.

17 > 14

greatest

14

17

22

26

31

31 is the greatest.

- **group**

Two pears are moved to make a group of 10.

- **half-circle**

- **half hour**

See **half past**.

- **half of**

One half of a square is shaded.

- **half past**

When the minute hand is at 6, tell the time as half past the hour.

The time is half past 7.

- **halves**

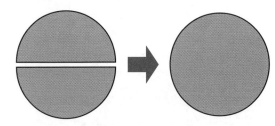

Two halves make a whole.

- **hour hand**

The hour hand is the short hand on the clock.

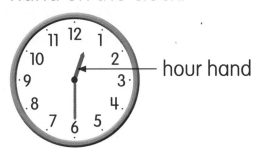

hour hand

L

least

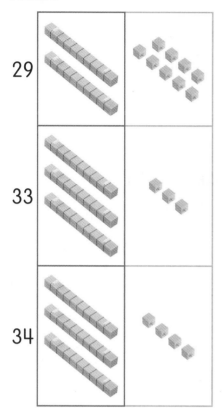

29

33

34

29 is the least.

less than

2 less

12 is 2 less than 14.

less than (<)

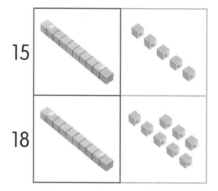

15

18

15 is less than 18.

15 < 18

M

minute hand

The minute hand is the long hand on the clock.

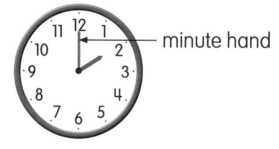

minute hand

months

There are 12 months in a year.

more

There are more zebras than elephants.

more than

13 is 2 more than 11.

N

number bond

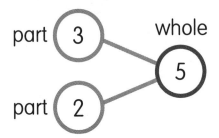

A number bond shows parts and the whole.
Parts make up a whole.

O

o'clock

When the minute hand is at 12, read the time as o'clock.

The time is 1 o'clock.

P

- **part**

  See **number bond**.

- **place value**

  The numbers from 11 to 40 are made up of tens and ones.
  12 = 1 ten 2 ones
  35 = 3 tens 5 ones

- **place-value chart**

  A place-value chart shows how many tens and ones are in a number.

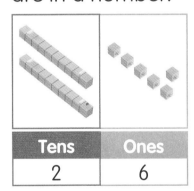

Tens	Ones
2	6

  26 = 2 tens 6 ones

- **pyramid**

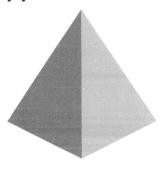

Q

- **quarter-circle**

- **quarters**

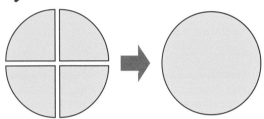

  Four quarters make a whole.

- **quarter of**

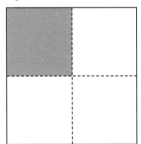

  A quarter of the square is shaded.

R

- **rectangular prism**

Glossary **447**

© 2020 Marshall Cavendish Education Pte Ltd

repeating pattern

A pattern that repeats again and again …

Circle, triangle, circle, triangle, ...

S

same

The number of cats and balls is the same.

seasons

There are four seasons in one year.

The seasons are spring, summer, fall, and winter.

T

thirty

Count	Number	Word
	30	thirty

trapezoid

- **true**

  $5 + 4 = 9$ is a true number sentence.

- **twenty-one**

Count	Number	Word
	21	twenty-one

- **twenty-two**

Count	Number	Word
	22	twenty-two

- **twenty-three**

Count	Number	Word
	23	twenty-three

- **twenty-four**

Count	Number	Word
	24	twenty-four

- **twenty-five**

Count	Number	Word
	25	twenty-five

- **twenty-six**

Count	Number	Word
	26	twenty-six

twenty-seven

Count	Number	Word
	27	twenty-seven

twenty-eight

Count	Number	Word
	28	twenty-eight

twenty-nine

Count	Number	Word
	29	twenty-nine

W

- **warmer**

- **weeks**

  See **days**.

- **whole**

  See **number bond**.

Y

- **year**

  See **months**.

Index

Pages in **boldface** type show where a term is introduced.

Cylinders, *throughout, see for example,* 138, 162–164, 166, 179–180, 200
    pictorial representation, *throughout, see for example,* 138, 164, 166–167, 169, 200

Date, **407**–408, 412, 431, 436, 439

Days, **402**–408, 410–412, 429–432

Different, *throughout, see for example,* 143, 148–151, 155, 161, 165

Digital clocks, **416**–417, 421, 425–426
    pictorial representation, 416–417, 420, 425–426, 428–429, 432

Divide, **152**–154, 160, 211

Doubles facts, **288**–291, 333, 335
    adding, 288, 290, 297, 333

Doubles plus one facts, 288, **289**–291, 335
    adding, 288, 290, 333

Equal, *throughout, see for example,* 58, 80, 115, 244–245, 370–372

Fact families, *throughout, see for example,* **108**–110, 126, 135, 277–278, 305–306

False, *throughout, see for example,* **114**–115, 119–120, 126, 312–313, 329

Fewer, *throughout, see for example,* **18**–21, 67, 271, 366–369, 389

Flat shapes, *throughout, see for example,* 142–143, 146–147, 172, 174, 176

Forty, **353,** 357, 386

Fourth of, **154**, 157–158, 207, 211

Fourths, **154**

Geoboards, 146

Geometric solids, *throughout, see for example,* 163, 165–166, 168, 177, 179

Greater, *throughout, see for example,* 21–23, 85, 243–245, 366–370, 373–374

Greater than (>), **244**, 370

Greatest, *throughout, see for example,* **245**–246, 264, 349–350, 372–375, 386

Group, *throughout, see for example,* 238–239, 284–285, 304, 316, 336
    adding, **284**
    subtracting, 303–304

Half of, **152**–153, 157–158, 207, 211, 220

Halves, *throughout, see for example,* **152**–153, 155–158, 160

Half-circles, *throughout, see for example,* **152**, 154, 176, 182, 207
    pictorial representation, *throughout, see for example,* 152, 155–156, 159–160, 172–174, 207

Half hour, **422**–423, 425–426, 432

Half past, **422**, 425–426, 429, 432–433, 436

Hour, 413–417, 430, 432–433, 436

Hour hand, *throughout, see for example,* **414**, 420, 422, 428, 430

Least, *throughout, see for example,* **245**–246, 264, 349–350, 373–375, 386

Less, *throughout, see for example,* 21–23, 28, 225, 247, 253–254

Less than (<), **244**, 371–372

Math balance, 53–54, 123

Manipulative
    attribute block trays, *see* Attribute block trays
    base-ten blocks, *see* Base-ten blocks
    base-ten rod, *see* Base-ten rod
    base ten unit, *see* Base-ten unit
    clocks, 413, 416, 421
    connecting cubes, *see* Connecting cubes
    craft sticks, *see* Craft sticks
    geoboards, *see* Geoboards
    geometric solids, *see* Geometric solids
    math balance, *see* Math balance
    ten-sided die, *see* Ten-sided die
    transparent counters, *see* Transparent counters

Minus, 80

Minute hand, *throughout, see for example,* **414**, 420, 422, 428, 430

Months, **402,** 404–412, 432–434, 439

More, *throughout, see for example,* 28–30, 48, 251–252, 368–369, 376–377

Morning, 419, 422–423, 427, 429

Night, 423, 427, 429–430

Number bonds, *throughout, see for example,* 49–56, 86–87, 274–277, 308–310, 318
    pictorial representation, *throughout, see for example,* 49–56, 86–87, 274–280, 303–313, 342

Number trains, *throughout, see for example,* 21–22, 28–29, 30, 246, 293

Numbers
    comparing, *see* Comparison
    ordering, *see* Ordering
    ordinal, 398–400
    patterns, *throughout, see for example,* 30–34, 37–38, 255–257, 259–260, 375–378
    place value, *see* Place value
    same, *throughout, see for example,* 2–4, **18**, 25, 53, 258

O'clock, *throughout, see for example,* 413, **414**–416, 418–419, 422, 432

Ones, *throughout, see for example,* 238–242, 244–248, 264, 360–364, 370–373

Ordering, *throughout, see for example,* 244–248, 250, 264, 349–350, 373–375

Ordinal numbers, 398–400

Patterns
    number, *throughout, see for example,* 30–34, 37–38, 255–257, 259–260, 375–378
    repeating, **194**, 200
    shape, *throughout, see for example,* 195–199, 201, 203, 207–208, 213–214

Part, *throughout, see for example,* **50**, 58, 68, 274, 276

Pictorial representations
    circles, *see* Circles
    clocks, *see* Clocks
    cones, *see* Cones
    counting tapes, *see* Counting tapes
    cube, *see* Cubes
    cylinders, *see* Cylinders
    digital clocks, *see* Digital clocks
    half-circles, *see* Half-circles
    number bonds, *see* Number bonds
    place-value charts, *see* Place-value charts
    pyramids, *see* Pyramids
    quarter-circles, *see* Quarter-circles
    rectangles, *see* Rectangles
    rectangular prisms, *see* Rectangular Prisms
    spheres, *see* Spheres
    squares, *see* Squares
    trapezoids, *see* Trapezoids
    triangles, *see* Triangles

Place value, *throughout, see for example,* **238**–240, 244, 246–247, 360–362, 386
    comparing and ordering, 244, 246–247

Place-value charts, *throughout, see for example*, 237–**238,** 271, 348, 359, 361
    pictorial representation, *throughout, see for example*, 237–238, 240–242, 244–248, 359–364, 386

Plus, 58

Pyramids, *throughout, see for example*, **162**–163, 169, 179–180, 183–184, 208
    pictorial representation 161–162, 164, 166–167, 169–170, 207

Quarters, **153**–154, 156–157, 160, 207

Quarter-circles, **153**–154, 159, 207
    pictorial representation, *throughout, see for example*, 153, 155, 157, 172–174, 207

Real-world problems
    adding, 74–75, 124, 322–323, 333
    subtracting, 102–103, 125, 322–323, 334

Rectangles, *throughout, see for example*, 138, 140, 142, 148–149, 185, 207
    pictorial representation, *throughout, see for example*, 138–140, 142–146, 172–176, 194, 207

Rectangular prisms, *throughout, see for example*, **162**–163, 166, 169, 179–180, 208
    pictorial representation, *throughout, see for example*, 161–162, 169, 188, 202, 208

Repeating patterns, **194**, 200

Roll, *throughout, see for example*, 165–167, 170, 208, 212, 216

Same, *throughout, see for example*, 24, 108, 114–115, 126, 245
    number, *throughout, see for example*, 2–4, **18**, 25, 53, 258

Seasons, *throughout, see for example*, 408, **409**–410, 412, 432, 434–435

Shapes,
    flat, *throughout, see for example*, 142–143, 146–147, 172, 174
    patterns, *throughout, see for example*, 195–199, 201, 203, 207–208, 213–214
    repeating, **194**, 200
    solid, *throughout, see for example*, 161–167, 169–170, 177–180, 183–184, 188
    sort, 149–151, 160, 167, 206–207, 210

Sides, *throughout, see for example*, **146**–148, 150, 159, 168, 188

Slide, *throughout, see for example*, 161, 165–167, 170, 208, 212

Solid shapes, *throughout, see for example*, 161–167, 169–170, 177–180, 183–184, 188

Spheres, *throughout, see for example*, 138, 162–163, 166, 179–180, 208
    pictorial representation, *throughout, see for example*, 138–139, 161–162, 166–167, 203, 208

Squares, *throughout, see for example*, 138, 141–144, 148, 152–154, 207
    pictorial representation, *throughout, see for example*, 138–140, 148–151, 171–176, 193–194, 207

Stack, *throughout, see for example*, 161, 165–167, 170, 208, 212

Subtraction, *throughout, see for example*, 80, 84–85, 302–305, 308–309, 376
    counting back, 85, 125, 276, 300–302, 334
    counting on, 82, 84, 125
    grouping, 303–304
    making a 10, 334
    real-world problems, 102–104, 125, 322–324, 334
    sentences, *throughout, see for example*, 80–81, 111–112, 276–280, 301, 306
    taking away, 80–81
    within 10,
      125, 276
    within 20,
      334

Take away, 79–81
    subtracting, 80–81

Ten, *throughout, see for example*, 237–238, 240–242,
    244–248, 264, 359–364

Ten-sided die, 308

Thirty, **353,** 386

Time
    half hour, *see* Half hour
    half past, *see* Half past
    hour, *see* Hour
    hour hand, *see* Hour hand

Transparent counters, *throughout, see for example*, 19,
    29–30, 285–286, 304, 351

Trapezoids, *throughout, see for example*, **142**–145, 148,
    159, 176–177, 207
    pictorial representation, *throughout, see for
        example*, 142–146, 148–151, 172–176, 193–194,
        207

Triangles, *throughout, see for example*, 138, 142, 153,
    176–177, 207
    pictorial representation, *throughout, see for
        example*, 138–139, 142–146, 155, 172–176, 207

True, *throughout, see for example*, **114**–115, 126, 132,
    312–313, 334

Twenty-one, **352**, 386

Twenty-two, **352**, 386

Twenty-three, 386

Twenty-four, 386

Twenty-five, 386

Twenty-six, 386

Twenty-seven, 386

Twenty-eight, 386

Twenty-nine, 386

Warmer, **409**

Weeks, **402**–404, 411–412, 432–434, 436, 439

Whole, *throughout, see for example*, **50**, 58, 68,
    274, 276

Year, **402**, 404–412, 432–434

Photo Credits

© Yvdavyd/Dreamstime.com, ii) © anna1311/Think Stock/iStock, iii) © Pichest Boonpanchua/Dreamstime.com, iv) © Buppha Wuttifery/Dreamstime.com, v) © anna1311/iStock, 230m: © MCE. Objects sponsored by Noble International Pte Ltd., 231t: © Tinarayna/Dreamstime.com, 232: © piotr_pabijian/Shutter Stock, 233t: © Pattra Jayasvasti/Think Stock/iStock, 233m: © boule13/Think Stock/iStock, 233b: © MCE. Objects sponsored by Noble International Pte Ltd., 235m: © MCE. Objects sponsored by Noble International Pte Ltd., 236b: © MCE. Objects sponsored by Noble International Pte Ltd., 238(t to m): © Exopixel/Dreamstime.com, 238b: © MCE. Objects sponsored by Noble International Pte Ltd., 239: © MCE. Objects sponsored by Noble International Pte Ltd., 240(t to b): i) © Exopixel/Dreamstime.com, ii) © MCE. Objects sponsored by Noble International Pte Ltd., iii) © Alexan24/Dreamstime.com, iv) © MCE. Objects sponsored by Noble International Pte Ltd., 241t: © vincomfoto/iStock, 243b: © MCE. Objects sponsored by Noble International Pte Ltd., 244t: © MCE. Objects sponsored by Noble International Pte Ltd., 246m: © MCE. Objects sponsored by Noble International Pte Ltd., 249t: © Motorolka/Dreamstime.com, 249m: © Aliaksei Smalenski/Dreamstime.com, 251: © MCE. Objects sponsored by Noble International Pte Ltd., 252: © MCE. Objects sponsored by Noble International Pte Ltd., 253: © MCE. Objects sponsored by Noble International Pte Ltd., 254: © MCE. Objects sponsored by Noble International Pte Ltd., 258: © MCE. Objects sponsored by Noble International Pte Ltd., 261: Created by Fwstudio - Freepik.com, 265t: © anna1311/iStock, 265m: © Witoon Buttre/Dreamstime.com, 266m: © MCE, 269: © Elena Schweitzer/Dreamstime.com, 269t: © Paradoks_blizanaca/Dreamstime.com, 273: © silvae/Shutter Stock, 278: © MCE. Objects sponsored by Noble International Pte Ltd., 282ml: © nicescene/Think Stock/iStock, 282mr: © Panupong Ponchai/Dreamstime.com, 282br: © Elena Schweitzer/Dreamstime.com, 283t: © Panupong Ponchai/Dreamstime.com, 283b: © MCE. Objects sponsored by Noble International Pte Ltd., 284: © andreahast/123rf.com, 285: © MCE, 286t: © Phive2015/Dreamstime.com, 286b: © MCE, 287b: © MCE, 288: © MCE. Objects sponsored by Noble International Pte Ltd., 289t: © MCE, 290: © MCE, 291t: © MCE. Objects sponsored by Noble International Pte Ltd., 292: © MCE. Objects sponsored by Noble

International Pte Ltd., 293: © MCE. Objects sponsored by Noble International Pte Ltd., 294: © MCE. Objects sponsored by Noble International Pte Ltd., 295t: © Daniel Padavona/Dreamstime.com, 295m: © Photozek07/Think Stock/iStock, 296(t to m): © yurakp/123rf.com, 296b: © MCE, 300t: © Alexei Sysoev/Dreamstime.com, 302t: © Jmad/Dreamstime.com, 303t: © MCE. Objects sponsored by Noble International Pte Ltd., 303(mr to br): © design56/Think Stock/iStock, 304m: © MCE, 306t: © ilietus/Think Stock/iStock, 306b: © MCE. Objects sponsored by Noble International Pte Ltd., 308: © MCE, 309m: © MCE, 310t: © Tikkirio/Dreamstime.com, 310m: © MCE, 311tl: © Anton Starikov/123rf.com, 311tr: © MCE, 312t: © MCE, 314: © piotr_pabijian/Shutter Stock, 315t: © anna1311/Think Stock/iStock, 315m: © Yvdavyd/Dreamstime.com, 315b: © MCE. Objects sponsored by Noble International Pte Ltd., 316b: © anna1311/Think Stock/iStock, 317t: © photomaru/Think Stock/iStock, 317m: © MCE, 321m: © Boonchuay1970/Think Stock/iStock, 321mr: © MCE. Objects sponsored by Noble International Pte Ltd., 321bl: © anna1311/Think Stock/iStock, 322: © MCE. Objects sponsored by Noble International Pte Ltd., 324t: © Tanapon Samphao/Dreamstime.com, 328b: © Witoon Buttre/Dreamstime.com, 329: © Created by Fwstudio - Freepik.com, 333mr: © Olga Popova/123rf.com, 324mr: © AlSimonov/Think Stock/iStock, 337b: © Anna Trefilova/123rf.com, 337b: © Benjamin Roesngsamran/123rf.com, 337b: © evaletova/123rf.com, 337b: © RTImages/Think Stock/iStock, 338t: © Yap Kee Chan/dreamstime.com, 339t: © Photozek07/Think Stock/iStock, 340: © Vvoevale/Dreamstime.com, 344tr: © Akabei/Think Stock/iStock, 345: © Akapelux/Dreamstime.com, 345tr: © Stas_V/Think Stock/iStock, 345ml: © Edgaras Kurauskas/Dreamstime.com, 345mr: © Elvira Gomolach/123rf.com, 345bl: © Maksym Bondarchuk/Dreamstime.com, 345bm: © cosmin4000/Think Stock/iStock, 345br: © tiero/123rf.com, 346t: © lleerogers/iStock, 346b: © Marusea Turcu/Dreamstime.com, 347m: © PhotoMelon/iStock, 347b: © ronniechua/Think Stock/iStock, 351m: © MCE. Objects sponsored by Noble International Pte Ltd., 351b: © MCE, 352: © MCE. Objects sponsored by Noble International Pte Ltd., 353b: © MCE, 354t: © Phanuwatn/Dreamstime.com, 355t: © Maksym Bondarchuk/Dreamstime.com, 355m: © Mustang_79/Think Stock/iStock, 355b: © cosmin4000/Think Stock/iStock, 356t: © Ekkapon/Think Stock/iStock, 356m: © anopdesignstock/iStock,

NOTES

NOTES

© 2020 Marshall Cavendish Education Pte Ltd

Published by Marshall Cavendish Education
Times Centre, 1 New Industrial Road, Singapore 536196
Customer Service Hotline: (65) 6213 9688
US Office Tel: (1-914) 332 8888 | Fax: (1-914) 332 8882
E-mail: cs@mceducation.com
Website: www.mceducation.com

Distributed by
Houghton Mifflin Harcourt
125 High Street
Boston, MA 02110
Tel: 617-351-5000
Website: www.hmhco.com/programs/math-in-focus

First published 2020

ISBN 978-0-358-10177-2

Printed in Singapore

3 4 5 6 7 8 9   1401   26 25 24 23 22 21
4500817080   B C D E F

The cover image shows a koala.
Koalas have soft, grey fur and a creamy-colored chest.
They can only be found in some parts of Australia.
Koalas live on eucalyptus trees and eat the leaves.
Koalas are not bears but marsupials.
Marsupials are animals that carry their young around safely inside a pouch.